ULTIMATE EXERCISE ROUTINES FOR RIDERS

Fitness That Fits a Horse-Crazy Lifestyle

■ ■ ■

Laura Crump Anderson

Certified Personal Trainer

Trafalgar Square
North Pomfret, Vermont

First published in 2022 by
Trafalgar Square Books
North Pomfret, Vermont 05053

Disclaimer of Liability
The author and publisher shall have neither liability nor responsibility to any person or entity with respect to any loss or damage caused or alleged to be caused directly or indirectly by the information contained in this book. While the book is as accurate as the author can make it, there may be errors, omissions, and inaccuracies.

Trafalgar Square Books encourages the use of approved safety helmets in all equestrian sports and activities.

Library of Congress Cataloging-in-Publication Data
Names: Anderson, Laura Crump, author.
Title: Ultimate exercise routines for riders : fitness that fits a horse-crazy lifestyle / Laura Crump Anderson.
Description: North Pomfret, Vermont : Trafalgar Square Books, 2022. | Includes index. | Summary: "Beginning with explanations of why strength, flexibility, and balance is important to achieve out of the tack, certified fitness trainer Laura Crump Anderson provides important rules and guidelines for stretching, weight training, and cardio to keep you safe. A lifelong equestrian herself, she then approaches the scheduling issue head-on, helping readers determine where best to fit in the minutes they need in the places they need to be anyway-the tack room, the arena, the barn aisle. Using only basic items you are likely to find around the stable, she keeps equipment needs straightforward, recognizing that the less likely it is you forget something, the more likely it is you'll get that workout in. Readers are then treated to seven original fitness routines, each dedicated to a specific area like the lower body or the core, or designated as a full-body program. Full color photos of top riders, including Jan Byyny, Sloane Coles, and Sharon White, demonstrate how to perform exercises effectively, and step-by-step instructions ensure you get it right"-- Provided by publisher.
Identifiers: LCCN 2021049401 (print) | LCCN 2021049402 (ebook) | ISBN 9781646010769 (paperback) | ISBN 9781646010776 (epub)
Subjects: LCSH: Horsemanship--Exercise. | Horsemanship--Health aspects. | Horsemen and horsewomen--Health and hygiene.
Classification: LCC RC1220.H67 A53 2022 (print) | LCC RC1220.H67 (ebook) | DDC 613.7/045088798--dc23/eng/20211109
LC record available at https://lccn.loc.gov/2021049401
LC ebook record available at https://lccn.loc.gov/2021049402

Photos by Laura Crump Anderson *except* Routine 8 and Yin Yoga Routines (by David Crump)
Book design by Lauryl Eddlemon
Cover design by RM Didier
Index by Andrea M. Jones (www.jonesliteraryservice.com)
Typeface: Myriad Pro

Printed in China

10 9 8 7 6 5 4 3 2 1

This book is dedicated to you,
the reader. You deserve the key to
unlock your fitness and riding goals.

■ ■ ■

Contents

Part 2: 8 Rider Exercise Routines 55

125

141

Preface

I have written this book to make clearer the murky waters of rider fitness. It is designed to fill in the gaps in our understanding related to rider fitness with *accessible* workouts. Riding is challenging, and believe me, you are one strong person for sticking with it. But maybe you picked this book up because you feel like you are lacking something. I'm going to tell you that you are actually doing *great*—what you learn in this book can just be the cherry on top.

Oftentimes we spend hours in the barn, dedicated to the care of our horses. But then we forget to take care of ourselves. We analyze the nutrition tag on our horses' grain, but thoughtlessly throw a pre-made meal into the microwave because we simple do not have time to cook or prep. Many times we have every intention of going to the gym but come home to discover that we are just too exhausted from a long day at work. The fact is, while riding is a very physical activity it does not lead to ideal fitness. This book helps you fill in the holes and move toward that "ideal" fitness. I also understand that while both the professional rider and the adult amateur deal with different kinds of time constrictions, time is always of the essence, so these pages will help you navigate fitness in an efficient way.

Rider fitness is something I have struggled with my whole life. My first experience in the saddle was before I was born. My mother was an enthusiastic equestrian who helped foster in me an extreme appreciation for both our equine partners and the robust athleticism required of top riders to stay in the game. I started riding in fields and trails on my first pony Starlight, who was so naughty that she would go under the fences of the riding arena to try and get out of work (with me on her). My determination was born on the back of that pony, and eventually I was cantering all the way around the arena. Starlight taught me how to stick with anything that was thrown at me. In my barn I developed a reputation for riding anything. I loved the thrill of getting a horse to do something that other riders had struggled with. This landed me in the dirt a lot. But the drive to always improve my skill and communicate with the horses in their language kept me going.

As a rider, I spent countless hours working on and improving my skills. Like others, I spent thousands of dollars every year to ensure that my horses were fit, sound, and ready to compete. But when it came to my own body, I often neglected my health to focus on making life better for my equine companions. By the time I was 14, I had already done irreparable damage to my body that I have since learned will be with me for the rest of my life.

If instead we treat ourselves like the athletes we are, we can extend our riding journey and make the most of our time on horseback. Too many in our community have ended up with chronic injuries that impair their ability to be effective riders and to do what they love. Our horses deserve riders who take care of themselves with the same level of respect that they care for their horses. Though underappreciated and under-discussed, rider fitness is critically important to your performance, your safety, and your ability to effectively communicate with your horse.

That's why this book is dedicated to you. It is time to give you the key to unlock your fitness and riding goals. Going to the gym is time-consuming and can be overwhelming, so in these pages I am giving you exercises that you can do in your own home or barn. Stick with it and stay strong!

Exercise Routine Models

Routine 1: **Jan Byyny**

Routine 2: **Sloane Coles**

Routine 3: **Rachael Livermore**

Routine 4: **Sharon White**

Routine 5: **Lauren Sprieser**

Routine 6: **Kara Doyle**

Routine 7: **Kaitlin Clasing**

Routine 8 and Yin Pose Routines: **Laura Crump Anderson**

Introduction

Get Fit—and Stay Fit—for the Sport You Love

All too often, my clients tell me that the number one barrier to exercise is a lack of time. Between horses, competitions, family, careers, and other obligations of daily life, many riders are already overloaded. How can they possibly shift their priorities to fit yet another thing into the mix? I get it; everyone is busy. But to be frank, this mindset is horseshit.

As riders, we know it takes countless hours to develop our skills. We have no qualms about spending precious time and money on training and conditioning, having the proper equipment, and optimizing nutrition for our horses. However, our own bodies are too frequently an afterthought. Rider fitness is important for many reasons including improved safety, greater connection with your horse, and treating yourself like the athlete you expect your horse to be. Despite what the skeptics in your family might say, riding *is* a sport and simply by participating in it you *are* an athlete. It's time to start acting like one.

If you want to ride at peak performance for as long as possible, finding an effective exercise program that fits your life can't just be wishful thinking; *it's absolutely imperative*. The longer you delay, the faster your body will start to fall apart. Trust me when I say, it happens faster than you might think. When I was 14, I was told that I had the spine of a 90-year-old by an orthopedic surgeon. This was from not only the abuse of hitting the ground many times but also from the wear and tear of lifting heavy water buckets and wheelbarrows improperly and excessively.

I was very much of the mindset of "fit it in" to make one less load to carry! This led to chronic back pain that I still live with, to this day, now more than 15 years later, and is proof that you do not have to be jumping massive fences or starting young horses to get injured riding. Actually, fitness-related injuries are often incurred while mounting and dismounting, and can happen on even the most bombproof of horses.

So we need to recognize that poor rider fitness leads to injury or making costly mistakes. When you are fatigued, you are more likely to take a risk that you would not have taken otherwise—for example, going for the "long spot" when it really is not there. Not only are strong bodies less prone to breaking down and more able to withstand the impacts of riding, but also the habit of working at a high intensity *out* of the tack makes you more clear-headed when you have to make a quick decision *in* the tack because your body is used to being at a heightened state of awareness and performance.

And, it is a fact that when you are unfit you are more likely to encounter pain. Exercising regularly helps keeps aches at bay. I experience this personally: If I skip a day of working out I may not feel it, but if I go a week without my regular exercise routines, I really start to feel stiff and hurt in ways that I would not feel otherwise. When more than a week goes by of missed exercise (I am human…it happens!), I really start to feel pain impact the way I move on a regular basis, and I can imagine that my horse notices the difference.

The Costs of Poor Rider Fitness

We only get one body in this lifetime. But that's not always how we behave. Instead, we act like we can just upgrade to a new body when we've worn the old one out. It is important to put premium fuel in our bodies in the way that we eat. It is also important to exercise regularly because our bodies need to be cared for like the precious vehicles they are. When I was younger, I would lie in bed, unable to sleep because I was in so much physical pain. My upper back cracks and pops like a meat grinder to this day. As a young rider, I thought I was invincible. It was a rude awakening to come to realize that physical pain was something I would suffer from for the rest of my life—all because I treated my body like it was replaceable. I did not listen to the constant signals to *slow down*.

I have also seen the long-term physical

effects of a life with horses on others. As good horse owners, we never complain about stacking hay, lugging water buckets or grain bags, cleaning stalls, fixing fences, longeing this horse, wrapping that one, and making sure our horses generally get adequate exercise and care. *But our bodies do*. I have worked with professional-level riders who are dealing with injuries so intense they are unable to feel certain parts of their bodies. They keep going and perform at the top level of the sport—injuries do not have to be the end of a career, but they are a handicap, and they impact your ability to perform at your best.

And life with horses is inherently dangerous. It is simply impossible to eliminate the risk that arises when you swing your leg over an animal that weighs a thousand pounds or more. I've never met a horseperson who hasn't been kicked, stepped on, jumped on, bitten, squashed against a stall wall, dragged, dumped, or all of these—to a certain extent, it comes with the territory. However, poor rider fitness enhances the dangers we come to expect in our work with horses, increasing the likelihood of accidents or of minor injuries developing into chronic pain that never goes away.

Fatigue is another symptom of lack of fitness whose danger we fail to appreciate. As I've already mentioned, it can lead you to go for the long spot when the right decision is to take the closer distance at a fence; to lose focus in your dressage test, giving late or lazy aids that confuse or irritate your horse; or to take a spill when greater endurance might have allowed you to stick on. This happens not only because your body is losing steam, but also because your brain is compensating for the exhaustion you are experiencing. Simply put, when you're tired, you are not performing at your best. Improving your fitness overall will decrease fatigue, and fatigue-related problems, while riding.

Although one of the best ways to build riding stamina is through time in the tack, *cross-training* dramatically improves your strength, flexibility, and aerobic capacity, which all contribute to fitness, focus, and a more sustainable position. Cross-training also improves your coordination and reaction time, allowing you to think quickly when you need to get out of tricky situations. The right type and frequency of exercise can improve your proprioception—the body's ability to sense where it is in space—leading to improved coordination and ability to precisely and concurrently use different body parts.

I'm sure I don't have to tell you how important clear non-verbal communication is with your horse—it's all we've got in our quest to get an animal who is 10 times our weight to do what we ask! Timing is everything when it comes to training horses effectively. If you react a second too late, often the opportunity for clarity, correction, or true harmony and synchronization has passed. That's why improving your coordination, even by small degrees, improves your connection with your horse. Building a strong signal between you and your horse is imperative to success. Without it, you will not be able to keep up with the physical and mental demands of riding. When you are strong, flexible, and aerobically fit, however, the likelihood that your horse will understand your aids increases dramatically.

Most fitness programs are not designed to meet the specific needs of riders.

Lack of Fitness Holds You Back from Reaching Your Full Potential

Why do we neglect our health as riders when doing so causes all of the problems I've mentioned and more—and could even keep us out of the saddle for good? As we've discussed, *not having enough time for exercise* is the number one excuse I hear from clients. I get it—we are all busier than ever. And if we could somehow find the time, it's hard to know which types of exercise will have the greatest impact on our abilities in the saddle and on the ground with our horses. Most fitness programs are not designed to meet the specific needs of riders, and even if you hire a personal trainer, most of them do not have experience with horses and do not understand the particular strengths and weaknesses we tend to develop in the tack. (Personal trainers are also expensive—I know because I am one!)

In our perpetual time crunch, we also tend to want to devote every spare moment we have to horse care and riding. There is always more work to do at the barn. And beyond that, it's fun! Why else would we work so hard? Quality time with our horses is what we live for: it's relaxing (most of the time!) and a source of great joy and fulfillment.

We're also taught that time in the tack is paramount, that it's the only thing that will really help us improve our skills as riders. Although nothing can replace experience in the saddle, and any rider fitness program should obviously have riding at its center, riding and caring for your horse alone will never be enough to keep you fit for a lifetime of peak riding performance. In fact, I am of the somewhat controversial opinion that while riding is obviously a physical activity, it does not actually count as *exercise*. Exercise is the act of moving the body in a way that is intended to build or maintain physical fitness, health, and wellness. We do not ride to stay fit, we ride because we enjoy it. You clean your barn because it must be done, not as a means to improve your physique. Although riding does provide a good aerobic workout, which is a key component of my fitness program (as we'll discuss in more detail later in the book) and doing chores has some physical and mental side-benefits, in many cases, these activities can actually lead to overall degradation of the body—the exact opposite of why we exercise.

In general, I think it's safe to say that rider fitness is undervalued as a factor in our overall performance, safety, and effectiveness at communicating with our horses. For most of us, it is an afterthought…or not even a thought at all. However, doing the right cross-training exercises out of the tack—like the ones I share in this book—can improve connection, coordination, reflexes, precision of the aids, strength, overall energy, and stamina to make you the best rider—and partner to your horse—you can be.

The Four Pillars of Rider Fitness

With the potential costs of poor rider fitness (see p. 2) and the many benefits associated with a fitter, healthier body, the question you should be asking yourself isn't "How can I make time for exercise in my busy life?" but "How can I afford *not* to make my fitness a priority?" In other words, the best you can do is reduce the risk of injury and muscle and joint degradation by undergoing a rigorous education in handling horses, always wearing a helmet, avoiding situations that you can't safely escape—and ensuring that you and your horse are as strong and fit as you can be. Effective exercise can go a long way toward mitigating the risks involved in equestrian sports by, as we've discussed, improving the rider's coordination, reflexes, strength, timing, and overall energy.

I've designed a holistic fitness program through years of experience working with riders like you that will 1) fit into your busy schedule, and 2) complement the excellent cardio you're already getting in the saddle with cross-training that will take your overall fitness and riding ability to the next level. As I've said, riding is the best way to get fit for riding, so *aerobic activity*, the natural outcome of your work in the tack, is the foundation (the first pillar) of my program. There are three other pillars that you'll need to integrate into your routine to support proper, well-rounded, and sustainable rider fitness: *strength training, stretching*, and *rest and recovery*. With this book as your guide, you'll learn about the basic building blocks of a weekly exercise program, based on these four pillars (which I discuss at length in the rest of Part I), that will help you stay fit and strong for years to come and improve your performance in the saddle—without interfering with your top priority: quality time with your horse.

Let's briefly look at each of the four pillars in turn.

Riding

There is no workaround. The best way to get fit for riding is with time spent in tack. You need to ride as much as you can. It is a bonus if you get the opportunity to ride as many different horses as you can. Even riding one horse five days a week beats hitting the treadmill for miles and miles. That said, if you are unable to make it to the barn most days of the week, you may need to incorporate additional low-impact aerobic activity or exercise that gets your heart rate up. In chapter 1 (p. 12), I discuss why riding is the first pillar of your rider fitness program.

Strength Training

You have to be strong to work with horses. If you did not already have considerable inner and outer strength, you never would have stuck with such a challenging passion past your first lead-line lessons. (And you definitely never would have picked up this book!) So pat yourself on the back, because I know you are strong already. In chapter 2 (p. 18), I'll talk about the basics of building muscle, how to increase your strength the right way, and how to improve the balance between strong and weak areas of the rider's body. Please note you *cannot* achieve a symmetrical body through riding alone. As riders, our inner thighs and hip adductors are very strong. Strengthening our *gluteus medius* out of the tack helps us develop a more "plugged-in" and connected sitting trot. No matter how many gallop sets you do or hours you spend on flatwork in the ring, it will never be enough to improve the strength across your chest. You need to do specific strength-training exercises off your horse to improve this area and balance out the strength of your upper back.

Past the age of 30, our bodies start to lose muscle mass. However, this is a natural process that you can actively work against. If you are looking for the Fountain of Youth, the answer is more muscle. Muscle is the most metabolically demanding tissue you can put on your body. Being "metabolically demanding" means that the more muscle you have on your body, the more calories you burn at rest. By increasing your muscle mass you: improve your ability to resist injury, improve insulin sensitivity (meaning, your blood sugar levels will stay more even), increase metabolism, improve body composition (meaning, you have less excess fat on your body), and so much more.

Losing muscle mass leads to a decrease in bone density. This is why strength training is an important measure in the prevention of osteopenia (when the body doesn't make new bone as quickly as it reabsorbs old bone) and osteoporosis (a condition in which the bones become brittle and frail). If you fight to combat the natural atrophy of aging with more muscle, you will live a longer, healthier life. And you will be able to ride your horses for longer.

Everyone has specific strengths and weaknesses; however, the sport we participate in tends to lead to universal imbalances in your body. For example, most riders have incredibly strong inner thighs: the *adductor longus*, *adductor magnus*, *adductor brevis*, *pectineus*, and *vastus medialis*. But their hip *abductors*, or the muscles that pull the legs *away* from the midline, tend to be incredibly underdeveloped: the *gluteus medius* and the *gluteus minimus*. Strengthening these muscles can lead to improvements in control and connection, making actions such as the sitting trot easier. Through the exercises in this book, you will learn to build upon the strength you already have (like in your inner thighs) and fortify the areas that are chronically weak (like the abductors). In the process, you'll safeguard your body against injury, improve your fitness in the saddle, and enhance your physical health for the long-term.

Stretching

Stretching is important because it takes care of our connective tissues and fascia. In chapter 3 (p. 26), I will discuss the importance of stretching in a format of *long static hold* that lasts at least three minutes. This type of stretching is practiced in yin yoga and activates the fascia to become more pliable and less sticky on top of itself. This leads you to feel lighter and less "stuck" in your movement.

I actually did not feel strongly about stretching until I started doing it regularly myself. I knew that strength training made me feel better and enabled me to move with less pain; stretching became the cherry on top because it enabled me to access movements that I'd previously found unattainable. It has allowed me to be more connected in my independent seat. I have been able to wrap my legs around my horse correctly. While muscular strength holds you in place, flexibility that is obtained by stretching enables you to access positions that are otherwise "bound up" or difficult for you. With my clients, I have noticed that by adding stretching routines to their weekly exercise protocols, the pain they live with is lessened. I also often advise clients to do additional stretching exercises on their own, and the impact in their riding is apparent. They are more able to connect with their horses through better aids and display less "noise" in their seat—instead of bouncing along, they become more "plugged in," creating a more harmonious picture. This is just as true for the adult amateur as it is for the professional rider. A regular stretching routine a couple of times a week really helps riders of *all levels* become more cohesive in their communication with their horses.

Rest and Recovery

The fourth pillar of rider fitness is probably the most overlooked part of any exercise routine. I, however, believe it is crucial, especially for the rider. Oftentimes riders wear the amount they are overworked as a badge of honor. You hear professional riders bragging about the number of days they have gone without a day off. Horses are a lot of hard work, but rest and recovery is an essential part of success because it allows your body to repair the damage done by all that hard work. A lack of rest and recovery leads to injury.

Oftentimes riders wear the amount they are over-worked as a badge of honor.

One of the most important parts of rest and recovery is ensuring you get enough sleep. The vast majority of the population requires eight to nine hours of sleep a night. Many people try to increase their productivity by cutting down on the number of hours they spend in bed, and this is a detrimental mistake because our bodies are designed to get a certain amount of rest and will begin

WE CAN'T IGNORE NUTRITION

I am not a nutritionist, but leaving nutrition out of the discussion on rider fitness altogether would be silly. What I advise my clients to do and what I practice myself at home is based on this simple rule: EAT REAL FOOD. This means food that comes out of the ground or had a mother. Pretty much everything else should be consumed sparingly. Give your body the nutrition it needs and it will perform miracles. Feed it crap and that's what you'll get in return. Don't think of "eating healthy" as being on some kind of diet; it's a way of living. Choosing the right foods will energize your body, enrich your life, reduce pain, and support your goals for achieving greater overall fitness for you and your horse.

With my busy schedule, I have always struggled to eat the right foods. The best tip I can give is to plan ahead, because once you are hungry the chance that you are going to make a healthy food decision is much slimmer. Instead, you are probably going to make the easiest choice that involves food that is right in front of you. So always have chopped vegetables that you like prepared in the fridge, but rotate them often so they do not go bad. Snacking is better for you when you have prepped fresh vegetables because the calories you are eating are less than, for example, chips, and you are eating *real* food. Planning is great way to avoid the mistake of eating poorly. This goes for cooking at home and eating out. When I go out to eat with friends I check the menu beforehand and decide what I am going to eat that meets the parameters of my "eat real food" rule. So when my friend orders a bacon cheeseburger with fries, I know already that I am getting the salmon salad with the vinaigrette dressing. While I may be tempted by the cheeseburger, I have made my decision previously with a clearer head and know I need to stick with it.

to perform at suboptimal levels when we restrict this integral aspect of our lives. In chapter 4 (p. 33) I discuss the importance of rest and recovery and suggest tips to ensure that you work this important part of any exercise program into your lifestyle.

I go into all the pillars in more detail in Part 1 ahead. Then, in Part 2, I'll get into the nuts and bolts of creating a weekly exercise schedule that includes each of the four pillars: I'll introduce the routines that will help you integrate cross-training into your busy life—and reap the benefits of better overall fitness, in the saddle and out.

Make Fitness a Priority

Riding is a team sport—you and your horse. We care about our horses, and in order for them to perform at their best, we have to perform at our best. But we can't do that if we continue to let rider fitness be our last priority. When I meet with clients for the first time, many of them have accepted pain as a regular part of their lives. It could be pain from an old injury, chronic muscle weakness, an overly tight muscle group, or from years of neglecting and abusing their bodies, often in the service of caring for their horses. And most of them know that pain is preventing them from being the best riders they can be: it affects their balance, the precision of their aids, their reaction time, and the overall harmony with their horses.

Some pain is unavoidable in the life of a horseperson. But while you can't prevent getting stepped on now and then, you can control your level of fitness and with it, your resilience and the odds of having a long and fulfilling riding career. I know you're busy—we all are. But the benefits of a fitter body are well worth the effort: you'll experience less pain, reduce the chance of injury, improve your strength, stamina, balance, focus, coordination, and connection with your horse—and have a better chance of bouncing back when inevitable injuries do occur.

The goal of this book is to help you fit a successful rider fitness program into even the busiest of schedules, and in the process, to help you improve your riding skills and communication with your horse *and* boost your health over the long-term. It's time to begin—if not now, when?

PART 1

WHAT TO KNOW BEFORE YOU BEGIN YOUR RIDER FITNESS PROGRAM

Starting a new fitness program can be very intimidating. Know that the exercise routines in this book are designed so that you can do them no matter what your fitness level is when you begin. You always have to start somewhere, so why not today just as you are?

It is important to get clearance from a doctor before beginning a fitness program, especially if you are recovering from an injury. I also believe you should be cleared by a physical therapist if you are coming back to riding or activity following an injury. A PT will be the best at determining if your body is ready to return to an exercise program and can ensure you are doing so without asymmetries that can lead to new problems down the road.

Just remember that setbacks will happen; you will not be perfect. If you are starting at the beginning of building your fitness level again, that is okay. Meet your body where it is today; do not compare your body to where it once was.

CHAPTER 1

The First Pillar of Rider Fitness: *Riding*

The first pillar of any rider fitness program is riding a horse. The best way to get better at riding is with time spent in the tack. It is also true, as I've already mentioned, that the best way to get fit for riding is by riding. While I can teach you exercises that can improve the strength of your legs, you cannot learn the muscle memory required to hold the galloping position without spending the hours in the saddle that are required to become an expert. There is nothing you can do off the horse that creates the muscle memory you get from riding a horse.

Anyone who has spent a significant amount of time in the saddle knows that riding has a significant aerobic component. The cardiovascular demands of working with the movement of a 1,000-pound animal are no joke. *Aerobic capacity* is defined as the highest amount of oxygen that your body can consume during maximal exercise that consists of large muscle groups. Studies have proven that a rider functions at the highest level of oxygen exchange. In other words, riding a show jumping course is very similar to an all-out sprint, aerobically speaking. However, there is no amount of sprinting, biking, or time on the elliptical machine that will improve your ability to ride a horse.

Sport-Specific Training

Sport-specific training is designed to improve athletic performance in a particular sport. Sprinting and weight-lifting (for example) can make a tennis player a better all-around athlete and may boost focus, hand-eye coordination, reaction time, and endurance—skills that certainly contribute to competitive play. But cross-training won't make a tennis player better at serving the ball. There's only one thing that can do that: practice at serving.

Many riders come to me with complaints about their galloping position or sitting trot. They ask if there are exercises that they can do off the horse that will make these common challenges easier to overcome. The honest truth is that you have to train for these activities in the tack. While you can develop some of the muscle groups involved (including agonist and antagonist pairs of complementary muscles) and increase your overall level of fitness and coordination through cross-training, improving your galloping position or sitting trot just takes time and hard work.

The galloping position—a crucial skill for success at the lower levels of eventing and impossible to do without at the upper levels—comes from a strong lower body and engaged core. While there are exercises you can do out of the tack to strengthen these muscle groups, there is no substitute for hours in the tack doing trot and canter sets to develop the coordination, muscular strength, and stamina to sustain a sturdy two-point position through a grueling cross-country course. The more you do it, the more balanced, comfortable, strong, and effective you will become.

Many upper-level dressage riders will sit the majority of a lesson or training session after they have warmed up at the posting trot. The sitting trot becomes almost second nature for them because they have developed the skill to the point of mastery. Now ask a seasoned dressage rider to hold a two-point position for 30 seconds and you may not find the same level of performance. The dressage rider simply hasn't put the time into practicing—and the same can be said about the sitting trot for many hunter-jumper riders. (If you struggle at the sitting trot, my advice is to take it slow rather than going full steam ahead. An untrained individual sitting the trot for extended periods will only lead to sore backs—for both horse and rider. Try giving it the interval-training treatment instead: Start by sitting three beats of the trot and posting for two. Increase the intervals over time, sitting for 30 seconds and posting for 10 seconds and so on. Work up to the point where you can sit the trot for minutes at a time.)

The good news is that every time you get on a horse, you're killing two birds with one stone. Not only are you getting sport-specific training in, you're also meeting your weekly requirements for aerobic activity, or what we call "steady state cardio" in my profession—that is, training at a continuous, moderate level of effort that can be sustained for a lengthy period of time. The American College of Sports Medicine (ACSM) recommends doing 30 minutes of aerobic exercise most days of the week. For the purposes of our rider fitness program, I'd like you to shoot for 30 minutes of cardio at least five times per week. (We'll review my recommendations on frequency for each of the four pillars in detail in chapter 5—see p. 41.) Riding a horse meets the definition of steady state cardio. So if you are riding regularly, you are already meeting this goal. And if you're not able to ride this frequently, you have a few choices: you can ride more (hooray!) or you can supplement whatever aerobic activity you do get in the saddle with other cardio—although all cardio is not created equal.

Keep Your Cardio Low-Impact

I want to take a minute here to stress that while there are many options for getting your cardio in, some types of cardio exercise are better for you than others. Running and other forms of high-impact exercise may come immediately to mind when you think of aerobic activity, but high-impact exercise puts a lot of strain on our bodies, and especially on our joints. I have known many riders who have done great damage to their knees, hips, and lower back pounding the pavement with running, all in the name of improving their performance on horseback. But the proof of improvement just isn't there. I'd rather save my body from the extra concussion caused by running—just as we try to prevent excessive concussion to our horses by limiting the amount of jumping or galloping they do—and keep my joints healthy for my first love: riding.

If you are a runner and want to keep running, more power to you. But there are a lot of low-impact options that will give you a great cardio workout while also sparing your joints. These include swimming, rowing, elliptical, cycling/spinning, and even walking. Personally, I find biking to be the most helpful. I do it on both a stationary bike and a road bike, depending on the weather and the time I have for cardio on a given day.

Your aerobic sessions do not have to be long: 20 or 30 minutes of getting your body moving will do. In working with a lot of busy clients, I've found that one of the best ways to squeeze an effective cardiovascular workout into a short period of time is to do *interval training*. Interval training is when you systematically disperse high intensity efforts into lower intensity or steady state cardio. The way I would recommend doing this is by following a traditional format of *one minute on, two minutes off*. Start with a warm-up at a comfortable pace for about three to five minutes, then go "all out" for one minute. "All out" could mean increasing the resistance on a machine or picking up your pace. Aim to get as close as you can to maximal effort, then come back down to your warm-up pace for two minutes. Repeat until you reach the 20-minute mark, then switch to a cool-down pace for about 5 minutes to allow your heart rate to drop slowly and your breathing to return to normal.

Improved Cardiovascular Function and Breathing

The good news is that when you are riding you are doing a textbook definition of traditional cardio or aerobic exercise, and many of you are already meeting the ACSM guidelines I mentioned earlier (30 minutes of moderate intensity exercise five days a week, and at least 20 minutes of vigorous

INVEST IN YOUR SHOES

While it is not uncommon for riders to drop hundreds of dollars on shoes for their horse every four to eight weeks, when it comes to our own base of support, we often settle for sneakers that are years old and were bought because of color or price.

But for horse and human athletes alike, our feet are what hold us up. The impact of your foot hitting the ground (or pressing into the stirrup) works all the way up the *kinetic chain* in your body. The concept of the kinetic chain says that, because the rigid parts of our skeletons are overlapping and connected, when one joint is in motion, it creates a chain of events that impact the movement of neighboring joints and body segments. So if your foot or ankle is encountering a harmful force, this impact will work its way up the kinetic chain through your knees, hips, and even your neck.

That's why it is important to buy the best footwear you can afford—shoes are not the place to cut corners. This goes for both your riding boots *and* your workout sneakers. I highly recommend finding an expert who can analyze your gait and help you find the correct shoe (and/or corrective insole) for you. Sneakers, like car or bike tires, do "go flat," so you should be purchasing a new pair every six months if you use them regularly (and hopefully after reading this book, you will be!)

exercise three days a week). Traditional cardio does not only get your heart rate up but also increases your respiration rate. Breathing is a very important part of any exercise program. This may sound obvious, but the circulation of oxygen through our bodies does a lot of work that flies under the radar. As you increase the demand of oxygen that your body is producing, your need to breath is going to increase. However, the tendency during intense exercise or when under pressure is to hold your breath. I know many of us can relate. Think of the last time you rode a dressage test in front of a judge or jumped around a cross-country course.

The tendency during intense exercise or when under pressure is to hold your breath.

▪ ▪ ▪

You need to fight this urge and learn proper breathing techniques. One of the best ways to accomplish this is to practice breathing in through your nose and out through your mouth. This helps decrease the chance of getting a "stitch" or cramp in your side.

The benefits of breathing while you exercise include:

- Being able to continue for longer periods, more comfortably and easily.
- Improved blood flow throughout your body.
- Improved ability to relax.
- Decreased chance of spiking your blood pressure and becoming nauseated.

In yoga there is something called *pranayama*, which is *breath work*. This is where you use focused breathing techniques to improve anything, from physical performance, to anxiety, to focus. There are many different breathing techniques, but I want to really focus on one. When we are stressed we tend to breathe in our chests. Where we really want to be breathing from is our bellies. This is really important because it properly engages the use of the *diaphragm*. The diaphragm is the dome-shaped muscle that I consider to be at the top of your core. It sits underneath the lungs. As you inhale, the dome of your diaphragm goes down toward the pelvic area, and as you exhale, it comes up under your rib cage. You can feel this by placing your hand just above your belly button: When you inhale your hand should go up and out, and as you exhale your hand should go down and in.

You can practice proper breathing

techniques while you are on the ground, but this is also something important to think about and practice in the tack.

Important...But Second in Line

Aerobic activity is the foundation of rider fitness. Lucky for us, we can satisfy most if not all of our weekly cardio requirement with our regular rides. In fact, as we've discussed at length in this chapter, the sport-specific training you do in the saddle is the only way you will ever master certain skills as a rider. In my opinion, you should spend as much time as you can in the tack, working on the things that you struggle with most, whether that's the sitting trot, seeing the right distance to a fence, fluid transitions, or the whole-body half-halt. We won't become well-rounded riders by staying in our comfort zones. If you're primarily a hunter-jumper rider, spend some time working on your sitting trot. And if you prefer dressage, don't neglect your two-point position.

If you are unable to ride five times a week, it is important to choose other low-impact forms of cardio exercise, such as cycling, rowing, swimming, or walking to protect your joints while reaping the many benefits of aerobic activity.

One thing to keep in mind is that although cardio is a very important part of any rider fitness program (riding is, after all, one of the four pillars of this program), it always comes second to strength training. If you can only fit in a couple of workouts a week, those sessions should be dedicated to strength training because that is where you get the best bang for your metabolic buck. If you do your strength training right and get your heart rate up as I discuss in the next chapter, you'll be getting in a decent cardio workout, too.

CHAPTER 2

The Second Pillar of Rider Fitness: *Strength Training*

The importance of muscle in your overall health cannot be overstated. There is a direct correlation between muscular strength and improved athletic performance. And that is why making your body stronger is the central focus of the rider fitness program in this book. As we discussed in the last chapter, the aerobic and sport-specific training that you are already doing in the saddle is your foundation—the baseline of both good rider fitness and development of your riding skills. But strength training is like an amplifier for your fitness: it turns everything up. Building muscle not only supports cardiovascular function, which helps you meet the demands of our very physical sport, it also reduces pain and improves your reflexes, coordination, ability to communicate with your horse, resistance to injury, and resilience when injury does occur.

Although riding horses naturally builds muscle, it also creates asymmetries, or strengths in some parts of the body and weaknesses in others. I have developed the routines in Part 2 through years of experience working with riders to help you balance out these common asymmetries and take your rider fitness to the next level, whatever that looks like for you. Like many people I know, you're probably cringing at the idea of dragging yourself to the gym to spend your precious time lifting heavy weights. But I believe that you can do a lot to build strength with very little equipment. So the exercises you will read about in the pages ahead are *body-weight exercises*—using your own body weight for resistance—that you can do from the comfort of your own home or at the barn. If you think the lack of equipment means the routines won't be challenging, think again: Body-weight exercises produce results as impressive as those you'd see from lifting weights in a gym. And research shows you only need to do strength training two times a week to reap all the benefits it offers. You have time for that!

Strength building might not be the most fun and exciting form of exercise. In fact, as I discuss later in this chapter, you will need to push yourself to the point where your muscles are fatigued deeply enough to make them stronger. This requires discipline and a willingness to keep going when you're bored, unmotivated, sore, or tired. But the health benefits of adding muscle mass are unparalleled. And while improvements to your performance in the saddle won't be instantaneous, within a couple of months in this program you will really feel a difference.

The Benefits of a Stronger Body

No matter how much muscle you build, you will never be strong enough to overpower your horse. The success of your partnership depends on your aptitude when it comes to nonverbal communication, and improving your strength *can* make you a more effective communicator, enabling more precise application and timing of the aids needed to make clear your commands. And the stronger you are, the easier it will be to lock into a methodical, independent seat, which is in constant communication with your horse about the correct rhythm, suppleness, connection, and impulsion.

Strength training out of the tack will also help you overcome two of the most common barriers to a healthy body and crystal-clear connection with your horse: pain and muscular asymmetry. When muscles are allowed to atrophy, the body becomes weaker, stiffer, and more likely to experience pain in general. And when we're in pain, we tend to compensate, often without knowing that we're doing it. Even seemingly minor adjustments made because you're hurting can scramble the signals between you and your horse.

I know a lot of riders who have struggled with pain in and out of the saddle. For instance, one woman I worked with suffered a series of injuries to her right leg—at the ankle and the hip—that made her left leg much stronger. As a result, her horse became overdeveloped on one side and underdeveloped on the other. Muscular asymmetry, whether due to pain or another cause, is a problem that crops up in a lot of riders. Both pain and muscular imbalances can interrupt your ability to communicate effectively with your horse and can even cause problems from efforts to compensate or work around deficiencies or discomfort. But building a stronger, more balanced body is within your reach. A big bonus is that increased muscular strength means you're less likely to experience pain in general.

Increased muscle mass actually acts as "armor," making your body more adept at withstanding the forces that cause injury.

Increased muscular strength also improves your metabolism and insulin sensitivity. High insulin sensitivity allows for the cells in your body to use blood glucose more effectively, reducing blood sugar. This leads to a healthier metabolism that is more able to fuel your body with the energy that it needs to be successful in the saddle.

Armor Up

Working to strengthen your body is a great way to defend yourself from injury in the first place. Muscle protects you in several ways. First, stronger bodies can react more quickly to dangerous circumstances—an unexpected spook or a stop at a fence, for example—in some cases averting disaster or at least minimizing the damage. We rarely know when danger is coming in our sport, so this is an important line of defense. More importantly, increased muscle mass actually acts as "armor," making your body more adept at withstanding the forces that cause injury. Thankfully, falls are fairly rare, but in the unfortunate case that you do part ways with you horse, a strong, fit body will fare better than a weaker one. (Learning how to fall correctly is a skill all its own, but that's a discussion for another book.) That's because muscle is much more resilient to trauma.

Strength training also improves bone density. This is because more muscle increases the amount of force placed on your bones every time you move. This triggers an increase in *osteoblast activity*, or the building up of new bone cells, and a decrease in *osteoclast activity*, or the process by which cells break down bone density. Increased bone density means stronger bones that are less prone to breaking, making the likelihood of walking away from an accident with minimal damage much greater.

Finally, building muscle tends to reduce recovery time when you do get injured.

There is no way to avoid the atrophy or muscle loss that comes with an extended period of recuperation. But when you are stronger prior to an accident, the body has a greater ability to supply oxygen to the areas that need to recover, and improved circulation means healing faster and getting back in the saddle sooner. I have known riders who have sustained some pretty serious falls. The ones who were incredibly strong *before* their falls were in much better shape afterward. The road back from a significant injury will always be long and arduous, but many riders at the highest level of the sport find their way back onto a horse, and many return to competitive sport successfully—*because* they are strong.

While it is incredibly rare, there is always the scenario of finding yourself in the hospital, fighting for your life. Should such a thing come to pass, you want as much muscular strength on your body as possible. This enables the doctors to give you every chance—going into major surgery as strong as possible ensures they can use all the tools in their tool belt.

The benefits of strength training for riders are clear and compelling. Stronger muscles translate to less pain, reduced muscular asymmetry, improved communication with your horse, stronger bones, greater protection against injury, and the resilience to bounce back if an accident does occur. Think of building muscle as preparing you for battle: You want to make sure your body is as strong as possible to defend against negative outcomes. But you will only realize these benefits under the right conditions.

Working to Failure

Momentary muscle failure sounds scary but reaching this point—the place at which you can no longer perform an exercise because you have fatigued your muscle so deeply—is actually the goal of strength training and a key feature of this exercise program. This state gives your body the opportunity to adapt and build more muscle in response to hitting its limit.

Momentary muscle failure is a simple concept to grasp. However, it is hard to achieve. In practice, it requires working through the burning sensation of muscle fatigue and really pushing yourself to the point at which you hit true failure, when your body is unable to continue. Plank is a great exercise for introducing yourself to this sensation:

1 Start on your hands and knees, then bend your arms and come down to rest on your elbows.

2 Extend both legs back so you are on your toes, maintaining a straight line from your head to your heels (Photo 1).

3 Hold the position for as long as you can. Your body will begin to shake but keep holding.

4 When you feel yourself reaching your limit and are just about to stop, count down from 10, holding the plank for just a little longer until you release the pose and allow your body to drop to the floor. This sensation, when you are holding the position despite your body telling you to stop, is what I want you to push for when you're doing the exercise routines in this book.

Although it sounds (and is) intense, momentary muscle failure can be achieved safely through extremely focused exercises (more on how to do this in the final section of this chapter, "Take It Slow"—see p. 24). In the case of our rider fitness program, think of failure as a stepping stone on the way to success—you need to fail in order to get stronger.

Workout Intensity vs. Duration

How long should your weight training sessions be? When it comes to building muscle, the intensity of your workout is actually far more important than the duration. It's the interplay between intensity and frequency—consistently pushing your muscles to the limits of their strength so they adapt and grow through high-intensity work—that will lead to results.

The goal of high-intensity strength training is to get your heart rate up quickly and keep it up throughout the workout. You should be working to a point where you experience difficulty breathing because the work you are doing is so challenging. A common way to identify the intensity of exercise is the *rate of perceived exertion* (or RPE). RPE is a universal language that is used by many fitness experts and amateurs alike. The RPE scale starts at 1, which is "no effort"—think of a leisurely walk or playing with your dog outside. Activities like riding fall in the middle where your breathing is elevated but you can still speak a full sentence. The scale ends at 10, which is all-out, maximum effort, like a sprint. Your strength training sessions should be conducted somewhere between an RPE 7 and an RPE 9, while hopefully spending more time closer to RPE 9.

As you progress in your workouts, you will get stronger and, therefore, the exercises that you are doing will get easier. When this happens, you need to up the intensity by increasing the amount of load you are applying to the muscles. This can be done in one of two ways: by increasing the amount of weight you are using or increasing the number of repetitions you are doing. The beauty of the routines in this book is that you can continue to increase the intensity of the same exercises almost indefinitely by doing more repetitions!

So, How Long Should My Workout Be?

As I said earlier, the duration of your workout is not nearly as important as the intensity of the workout. You can exercise for an hour on an elliptical machine and not get the benefits you need to be a better rider. Strength training for 20 minutes at a high intensity is a much more effective workout and will lead to a much stronger,

TO GET A TRAINER OR NOT GET A TRAINER—THAT IS THE QUESTION

Working with a personal trainer is a great way to improve your form and skill in a shorter period of time than it would take you on your own. The other great part about working with a trainer is she will usually get more effort out of you than you will be able to produce on your own. This leads to better results. Working with a professional is always a great option if a good one is available to you and you have the means to pay for it. While very few trainers have an understanding of the skill, strength, and cardiovascular effort that goes into riding a horse, that does not mean that you will not get a lot out of working with one. A good trainer will try to understand the demands of your sport and your time limits and build routines and programs that lead to improvement.

The biggest drawback of working with a trainer is the cost. You are paying for someone's expertise and this costs money. With care for your horse, riding lessons, and everything else that goes into our sport, sometimes it is hard to budget for an additional expense. That is where this book comes in. There is no reason you cannot get great results on your own. What you need is determination and the ability to stick with it. Remember that you will always be getting better results than the person who is not doing anything at all!

more balanced body and a dramatic boost to performance on horseback.

I think you'll like what I have to say next: You only need 30 minutes to get in a productive strength-building workout. In the amount of time it takes to watch a show on Netflix you could be making a huge difference in your fitness—a difference you and your horse will notice. And I know you want to be the best rider you can be for your horse—let that be your motivation. Getting started is often the most challenging part, so pick a time of day for your two, weekly strength-training sessions that works for you and stick with it. Keep in mind: These workouts are not supposed to be easy. You'll only achieve the results you want by maintaining a high level of intensity that keeps your heart rate up the entire time you're working out. You want to feel the burn in your muscles.

That said, working too intensely for too long is often where form starts to suffer and injury can occur, so keep your workout to 30 minutes or less in the optimal zone of 7 to 9 RPE.

Take It Slow

Moving slowly is a great way to build a strong, correct position in each exercise in your routine while also increasing intensity. When you complete a movement slowly you reduce momentum, requiring your muscles to do more work, which, in turn, gets you to the point of momentary muscle failure sooner. Moving slowly also allows you to focus on your form and ensure that you are doing each exercise accurately and to the full range of motion. While the intensity will build with each repetition, the amount of force applied to your muscles stays the same because you are moving at the same pace. Force is what leads to injury. A lot of the exercises that you do in this book will be done at a painfully slow pace, but resist the urge to rush through them because rushing will not produce the best results and could lead to injury.

I've said it before, but it bears repeating: When time is of the essence, strength training gives you the best return on your investment. And all you need is 30 minutes, twice a week. No gyms or equipment required, so no excuses. If you do nothing else after reading this book, I hope you will add these strength-training sessions to your schedule. In addition to the many benefits discussed in this chapter, building muscle is also an important weapon in the battle against aging. As we age, we naturally lose muscle, which leads to all kinds of problems. Through strength training, we can actually halt the atrophy process and build new muscle on the body.

One final note: I'm not saying you shouldn't work with weights. If you have the time, the skills, and the equipment, go for it. But there's a lot you can do with your own body weight in your own home or barn. The routines in Part 2 have been crafted over years of experience as a personal trainer working with busy riders to maximize results and minimize the chance of injury and the time required. Of course, the program works best when you put all four pillars together.

Let's talk stretching.

CHAPTER 3

The Third Pillar of Rider Fitness: *Stretching*

For the longest time, I ignored yoga and stretching in my own exercise regimen. While I knew on a practical level that stretching was an important aspect of fitness, I was never really drawn to it. But as the saying goes, when the student is ready, the teacher will appear. I have learned more about anatomy through my yoga practice then I have in any textbook. Through my yoga practice I was able to alleviate pain that I thought I would just have to live with for the rest of my life. Yoga has enabled me to be more present in my daily life and give me more power over my "racing thoughts" than any other form of exercise or medication.

Finding the right teacher is what convinced me of the benefits of yoga and stretching, and you might need to do the same to really get into it. But if the idea of attending a yoga class for the first time is intimidating (don't worry, I get it), or if you're a fan of yoga but struggle to fit regular trips to the studio into your busy schedule, I've put together a few sample sequences of yin poses (postures that are held for longer durations as you pay attention to your breath, thoughts, and physical sensations) customized for riders in Part 2 (see p. 136). As a certified yoga instructor, I've shared these, and other stretching poses, with clients and have seen great results. One adult amateur client has been strength training with me for a while. She was feeling stronger and more confident, but her riding instructor was not noticing much of difference in the saddle. We started incorporating long static holds (yin stretches) at the end of each workout, and within a month she was making noticeable improvement in her sitting trot. Her instructor, a busy professional herself and quite skeptical of the need for exercise outside of what regular riding and horse management requires, even started training with me after seeing the progress her "weekend warrior" was making.

Before we dive deeper into the benefits of stretching, I want to tell you a little bit about fascia.

Fascia

For many years fascia was thought of as inert tissue that just encased the muscles and organs and connected everything from skin to bones. With new science emerging all the time about fascia, it is funny to think that we ever assumed that something so pervasive had no greater purpose. In recent years, in fact, researches are debating whether fascia should replace skin as the largest organ in the body. Although fascia has been recognized in Eastern medicine as a key factor in our overall health and physiology for centuries, in the West, we are just beginning to understand the important role it plays.

Fascia is predominately made up of collagen, and is responsible for structure and lubrication of the tissues in the body. In her book *The New Anatomy of Rider Connection*, author Mary Wanless gives us a great way to think about fascia—she says to visualize an orange. The orange has an outer layer that protects it against the elements. The fruit's skin is like your skin. Underneath the skin, there is a white pith surrounding the orange. It is also the connective tissue that runs down the middle of the orange and separates the wedges and holds each little droplet of orange juice, preventing the orange from becoming a puddle at the bottom of the skin. That is how fascia works in the human body too: It wraps around every organ, muscle, muscle fiber, muscle cells, nerve cells, and it even encapsulates your blood vessels and encases your bones. The fascia network extends from your head to your toes. If you were able to remove everything from your body except the fascia you would still be fairly recognizable as yourself.

Fascia provides critical structural support throughout our bodies, so we must take good care of it, keeping it supple and healthy with a combination of hydration, diet, and beneficial traction through long static holds. If we do not, we are in trouble.

Painful Fascia

Most athletes do not retire because of muscular injuries, which heal in time; they retire because of joint and fascia problems. Bad knees, a bad back, or a bad hip tend to boil down to excessive restricting of the connective tissues—such as the fascia, cartilage, and tendons—caused by overuse, injury, surgery, insufficient activity, excessive manipulation (like working too vigorously with a foam roller), and dehydration. "Bunched up" fascia becomes sticky, stiff instead of malleable, and painful. Painful fascia will not function properly, manifesting, perhaps, as scar tissue or as a joint "clicking" or "popping." Scar tissue is bad because it is thick and not able to move as well as healthy fascia. The good news is that "motion is the lotion" that will get your fascia—and your body—back in working order.

How to Stretch

If we want to maintain the health of our fascia and joints we must exercise them, but not in the same way we exercise muscle. Muscle responds and adapts to repetitive motion while fascia responds to long static holds. That's where stretching comes in, and the yin stretches in yoga, in particular. Staying still in the same position for anywhere from three to five minutes increases the hyaluronic acid in the fascia network, which makes the "webbing" or "netting" more malleable where it has a tendency to get stuck. In each routine you complete in this book, there is at least one long, static hold at the end of the exercise routine to keep your fascia supple and stable. (Note that it is important *not* to stretch before you do strength-training exercise as doing so decreases the integrity of the muscle.) Longer stretches at the end of a workout are also great opportunities to practice mediation and mindfulness, which I discuss in chapter 4 (p. 33).

When you are stretching you are not actually stretching the connective tissue, you are stretching the muscle; however, stretching the muscle leads to changes in the connective tissue that makes it more pliable. You may feel a deep tug, ache, or even a fiery sensation. It's also possible that you will not feel much during the stretch but will get hit with a tingly sensation as the blood rushes back to the area when you come out of it. Be as still as possible in your yin stretches. You should never bounce. And don't hold stretches through sensations that are sharp, shooting, or that make it difficult to breathe. These are signs that you're doing too much and need to back off before you tear something.

Stretches that are less than 30 seconds tend to be ineffective. Holds that are 30 to 90 seconds are good for your muscles. Holds that are between 90 seconds and three minutes begin to target the fascia. Static holds that last longer than three minutes are considered *yin holds.* The sweet spot is a static hold that is held for three to five minutes. These really get into working the fascia. Holding a stretch for more than 12 minutes tends to be a waste of time. It's better to use that time to fit in two six-minute holds or three four-minute holds.

Starting any exercise program can be intimidating. It's worth noting that it's common for long yin poses to feel challenging, subtle, intense, luxurious, or boring. The interesting thing about this style of stretching is that you can go through all of these sensations during a single stretch. This is one of the reasons why we hold our yin postures for three minutes or more. Learn to listen to your body and feel the subtle adaptations over the course of a stretch. Feel each sensation and accept it as it is, resisting the urge to chase a harder or more intense stretch. That's rarely what your body needs.

Being still for three minutes can feel like torture as your brain is going a thousand miles a minute. But you can do it! Try using your time on the ground or a yoga mat as an opportunity to practice mindfulness, focusing on your breath (then you're killing two birds with one stone!). Every time you notice your mind wandering, return to an awareness of the rhythm of your breath.
The benefits of doing long, static stretches

TO KEEP FASCIA HEALTHY, YOU NEED TO HYDRATE

I am not a nutritionist but I can tell you that I follow the guideline of drinking half your body weight in ounces of water a day. So if you weigh 100 pounds, you need to drink 50 ounces of water a day. This is something I have gotten from motivational speaker and author Rachel Hollis, and I stick with the guideline daily. As far as food goes, foods made up of collagen are very beneficial for fascia. A really good source of collagen is bone broth—you can make your own in a crock pot. (Or do what I do, which is buy an organic ready-made version at your grocery store.)

two to three times a week are well worth the effort. You'll keep your fascia and joints healthy and supple, target any constricted tissue, reduce pain and inflammation by improving pliability and blood circulation, and increase your flexibility.

The Other Benefits of Stretching

Flexibility is the ability to move a joint through its full range of motion with ease. It is determined by your body's muscles and connective tissue. Flexibility is a good thing because it allows you to wrap your legs around the horse. It helps with shock absorption, so it is important in the lower back, or lumbar spine.

Improved flexibility is not just about improving range of motion, although this is an important piece of the fitness puzzle. Improved flexibility can also lead to greater postural stability, correct muscle imbalances, improve balance control, and make movement easier—all of which can have a direct impact on your position and effectiveness in the saddle. Flexibility is joint specific, so just because you have good range of motion and flexibility in your hips doesn't mean the same will be true of your ankles or knees. As riders we tend to be particularly tight in our glutes, hip flexors, and lower back, but an effective stretching program should address the whole body, targeting the major muscle and tendon units of the shoulder girdle, chest, neck, trunk, lower back, hips, posterior (back) of the legs, anterior (front) of the legs, and ankles. The yin sequences that I provide in Part 3 (see p. 136) incorporate stretches for each of these key areas. You can do full sessions dedicated to only stretching problem areas or sequences that include stretches for the whole body—it's your choice. Thinking about where your body feels tight or needs more flexibility is a good place to start. Targeted stretching will improve flexibility and lessen pain in problem spots and increase your effectiveness in the tack. (Note that *too much* flexibility is not necessarily a good thing, because it can lead to joint instability and dislocation.)

Targeted stretching will improve flexibility and lessen pain in problem spots and increase your effectiveness in the tack.

Beyond decreasing joint and fascia pain and helping you heal from an injury, improved flexibility can lead to a more independent seat as well. The elusive independent seat is two components: the ability to maintain balance while not being influenced by the movement of the horse, and the ability to move one part of your body independent of other parts. Improved flexibility allows the rider to really sink into and go with the horse's movement instead of "clamping down" on the saddle. This leads to a seat that is more capable of both adapting to and controlling the horse's movement. The independent seat is a key skill for riding at any level and is absolutely essential at advanced levels.

Try This

One great area for rider to target is the inner thigh. This area is always tight in riders, and this stretch offers the additional advantage of developing your seat muscles. The best way to target the inner thigh with a stretch is as follows:

1. Lie on your back and scoot your bottom as close to a wall as possible.

2. Extend your legs straight up the wall in front of you.

3. Bring your feet away from each other on the wall as wide as they will go.

4. Hold this yin pose for three to five minutes.

Coming Back After Injury

It's important to note that if you're coming back from an injury or want to address stiffness or soreness in a specific area, you'll need a combination of strengthening and stretching to heal. Say you have a bad back. Along with exercises to strengthen your back, such as leg lifts and planks, you should also incorporate long, static yin stretches that target the thick connective tissue that surrounds your lumbar spine. Doing forward folds along with back bends will flood the affected areas with *hyaluronan* (hyaluronic acid), which helps make the fascia more supple and less constricted.

Frequency of Stretching

Stretching once today will not magically improve your flexibility. You need to do it consistently over time and remain committed to the process. It takes months to become more flexible, and it takes work to maintain good flexibility. Although you do not need to stretch every day, tending to the fascia and the joints with long, static yin holds should be done at least two times a week. An easy way to meet this goal is by working it into your winding down routine at the end of the day. (It's especially beneficial to stretch after a long, hard day!) Stretching in a very slow, quiet fashion during this time is a great way to prepare yourself for sleep. You only need thirty minutes of stretching per session to keep your connective tissue healthy and pain-free.

As I've already mentioned, avoid stretching prior to strength training or riding—it actually decreases the integrity of the muscle, which can lead to injury. Stretching should be reserved for *after* strenuous exercise.

I provide additional support for working long stretches into your life by including them at the end of each high-intensity exercise routine in this book. Although these isolated stretches should not be considered a substitute for full yin sessions (examples of which you will find in Part 3—p. 136), this is a great way to cool down while also caring for your fascia and connective tissue.

CHAPTER 4

The Fourth Pillar of Rider Fitness: *Rest and Recovery*

When it comes to our horses, we always incorporate rest and recovery into their training schedules. But we tend to operate at full speed, 24/7 ourselves, forgetting that we need a break from time to time, too. Rest and recovery are a key part of the fitness puzzle and are so often neglected by busy riders that initially I wanted this chapter to come first, *before* the other pillars of riding, strength training, and stretching, to illustrate just how pivotal I think it is to a healthy life. Rest and recovery still comes first in my mind. Without it, you simply can't achieve optimal results from any of the exercises I recommend in this book.

If people are going to cut corners, this is the part of the program where it happens most often—who has the time to stop or slow down? But trust me when I say that this attitude will catch up with you sooner or later. Your body cannot maintain an all-out dash forever, and eventually you will trip and fall. This crash often shows up as burnout, sickness, injury, or days when you just can't function. Your body needs time to repair itself from the physical stress and exertion associated with the equestrian lifestyle and to make the most of the workouts in your rider fitness program.

There are many forms of rest and recovery, but in this chapter, I will focus on just a few of the most important, along with some of my favorites: getting proper sleep, doing enjoyable activities that take your mind off the daily grind, limiting smartphone use, and incorporating mindfulness and meditation into your life. The idea that you can keep going "until you drop" is an unhealthy one that many riders continue to believe is necessary to excel. When you don't get enough rest, however, you are actually doing a disservice to your horse because what he needs most is a fit, present, attentive, and effective partner.

There are many other benefits to keep in mind, as well. For instance, rest and recovery are absolutely crucial to the process of building muscle, which is at the core of the rider fitness program in this book. It's during periods of rest that muscle fiber actually grows, so you don't need to be stressing your muscles every single day to get results—in fact, you should be careful not to overdo it.

Your body needs down time to build, detoxify, and recharge.

There are several ways to satisfy your body's need for rest and recovery. Let's talk about my favorites.

Sleep

Perhaps the most important way of satisfying the body's need for rest and recovery is ensuring that you get enough sleep. There is no replacement for a good night's sleep, and lost sleep cannot be made up. If you don't keep up with it, you are fighting a losing battle. Research bears this out. Many hours have been spent in labs, especially by the United States Military, trying to figure out how humans can get less sleep and still function at full capacity. Time and time again, these studies have proven that sleep is essential and cannot be compromised—there's just no substitute.

Despite all the science demonstrating that we need a minimum of eight hours of sleep per night, many people still believe they can get by on six, five, or just a few hours of sleep. It has been said that up to a third of the American population gets less than the recommended amount of sleep each night. While many of these people probably believe they are the exception to the rule, they're wrong. Everyone should be striving to get eight hours of sleep a night because your body physically needs this time to rest and recover. This is especially true for riders because they are so physically active. While you are sleeping your brain is doing essential "maintenance and cleaning." Your body needs down time to build, detoxify, and recharge. How much sleep you get influences how much you eat and how efficiently our metabolism works. Perhaps most important to note: Sleep deprivation can lead to impulsivity, a dangerous impediment to working with unpredictable horses in the saddle or on the ground. Our safety, along with the safety of our horses and the people around us, depends largely on our ability to make smart decisions quickly—and good judgment starts with a good night's sleep.

Luckily, there are evidence-based tactics you can use to make sure that you're getting enough sleep. Start with setting a bedtime that you will adhere to every day. This should be based on when you intend to wake up in the morning—work backward eight hours to determine your optimal lights-out. Many studies have shown that the blue light from our devices not only inhibits our ability to fall asleep, it also impacts the quality of the sleep we do get. So eliminate screens from your routine an hour before you go to bed. Running a fan and making your bedroom as dark as you can also helps create the best conditions for sound, sufficient sleep.

Recharge with Activities You Enjoy

Rest and recovery is not just about getting proper sleep. It's also about finding enjoyable activities that recharge your body and mind. It can be really hard for riders to do this in particular because horses are often all-consuming. But it's important to find reliable ways of disconnecting from the daily grind and refilling your energy tanks. One activity that I have found many of my clients learn to enjoy is cooking. The time spent watching cooking shows or flipping through a cookbook can be therapeutic on its own. But you also get to be creative and to make something tangible, nourishing, and enjoyable for you and your family. From my point of view, it is even better if you're focusing on creating nutritious meals to support your fitness goals. I find that I and my clients are more likely to eat a meal that we have taken part in creating, and trying new foods and recipes, or exploring different culinary traditions can be a lot of fun.

Cooking isn't for everyone, of course, so maybe you'd prefer to recharge by reading, walking, needlepoint, journaling, or watching television (though I strongly discourage this last as a regular go-to, as technology in any form can be stimulating rather than relaxing). No one else can tell you what your recharge activities should be. It's something you must discover for yourself. If you have no idea where to start, pick an activity that you have always wanted to try. For me that was archery. Although I have never hunted, I find the act of pulling back a bow and hitting a target to be very gratifying after a long day. I've been surprised to find comfort and renewal in writing as well. I never thought that I would enjoy writing because I am very dyslexic and it isn't easy for me. But with time and practice, I have learned to get my stress out through writing (thank you to my amazing editors for being able to decode "Lauranese"!). I suggest you make a list of activities that you know help you relax and recharge, along with any new activities you'd like to try. Then start making your way through the list, testing the activities to find the stress relievers that work best for you.

Stop Scrolling Through Your News Feed

Smartphones have quickly become a central part of our lives and they're often our default form of distraction and downtime. However, although your body is usually still when you are on your cellphone, don't mistake using it for rest and recovery. It has been found that scrolling through your phone creates unhealthy neurochemical reactions in your brain that lead to increased inflammation, anxiety, and stress. Try to limit the use of your devices as much as possible—they aren't healthy and, as studies have now shown, can even be addictive.

Personally, I have noticed a big difference in how my body feels when I am excessively on my phone. I often compare myself to other people and the curated versions of their lives that appear on social platforms. On some level, I know I am seeing highlight reels, but it still leads me to feel inadequate by comparison. The impact on my mental state has an effect on my physical well-being.

The trick when scrolling through Facebook, Instagram, and other social media platforms is to remember that you are comparing your insides to other people outsides. You are unable to see the struggles that the people around you are going through. I'd like to emphasize that it is easier to tune out this "noise" if you skip the scrolling altogether and choose downtime activities that allow you to relax, exercise your creative muscles, express yourself, or just think. Moving your body in some way is a much better way to pass the time than engaging on social media. Get up and go for a walk, leaving your cellphone at home (or at least in your pocket). It can be too easy when you use your phone to listen to music to pull it out and start mindlessly scrolling, so watch out for that. The point is to get *off* your phone and start moving your body. This can reduce your stress, lower your heart rate, and give you a feeling of calm and steadiness that you will not get from social media.

Meditation and Mindfulness

You're probably sick of hearing advice about incorporating mindfulness and meditation into your life. But there's a reason these forms of rest and recharging are so commonly prescribed: They work. The benefits are widespread, proven—and compelling. Meditation has many benefits such as reducing stress, controlling anxiety, promoting emotional health, and lengthening attention span. From my perspective, no worthwhile health and exercise regimen is complete without meditation. In this fitness program, it isn't optional—it simply must be part of everyone's daily practice. Although it can be challenging to grasp the transformative power of meditation at first, remember that it is called a "practice" for a reason. So whether you're a beginner, a "dabbler," or someone who has meditated regularly in the past, now is as a good a time as any to start (or start again).

The easiest way to begin that I can think of is to practice while brushing your teeth. While this is more of a mindfulness exercise than formal meditation, it requires the same skills to focus on brushing your teeth for a full two minutes. Notice every time your mind wanders and then return to focusing on brushing your teeth. Make sure to set a timer—you don't realize how long two minutes actually is until you force yourself to focus on a particular task for that long. The connection with the present moment through becoming very conscious of it can lead to improved attention and feelings of contentment and security.

Through the mindfulness practice of brushing your teeth—or washing the dishes, folding laundry, cleaning tack, mucking stalls, preparing or eating meals, or bringing your focused attention to any other mundane task—you can work your way up to seated meditation. Find a comfortable spot on the ground or in a chair. You can close your eyes or keep them open—whatever feels best to you. Leaving them open can challenge your attention. Closing your eyes might feel uncomfortable at first, but with practice, it often leads to a better experience.

Work up to "sitting" for 15 minutes every day in a comfortable position, focusing on your breath. There are many different tricks to use your breath to train your focus on the present moment. One is to count your inhales for four seconds and your exhales for six seconds. Every time you notice your mind wander, return to focusing on the breath. Try not to be judgmental toward what pulled you away, but do identify it (sound, sensation, thought) and simply bring your attention back to your breath.

Benefits of Meditation

Stress causes an increase in the hormone cortisol. This can lead to inflammation in the body, impact your sleep, increase depression and anxiety, increase blood pressure, and contribute to fatigue and cloudy thinking. Meditation has been shown to reduce stress in individuals who practice regularly. Incorporating such a reliable form of stress reduction into your day is a great advantage to your health.

Improved attention leads to better progress when working with horses, on the ground and in the saddle.

Meditation also gives you an opportunity to process emotions that you are sitting with, and this leads to improved levels of *emotional intelligence* (the capacity to be aware of, control, and express your emotions and handle relationships with others). It helps control anxiety because you are able to better identify where negative feelings may be coming from. During meditation you are focusing on one thing for a prescribed period of time (mindfulness), and this can lead to an increase in your attention span. Improved attention leads to better progress when working with horses, on the ground and in the saddle.

I work with a professional rider who was always in her head before show jumping. This led her to make terrible mistakes because she would freeze up. Knowing the difference meditation has made in handling my own anxiety, I recommended she commit to regular practice and see what happens. She started to meditate regularly, including sitting before her show jumping round, and this led to better, more confident, consistent rounds. She experienced less anxiety before she went into the ring because she was feeling more centered and confident. My client now meditates for 10 minutes every day as part of her morning routine, whether there is a competition or not. She swears by the difference that it makes.

Visualization

Visualization is probably a focus and stress-reduction technique that is familiar to many riders already. But it can also be an important tool in your rest-and-recovery toolbox. I often use visualization when I am worried about an upcoming event. Taking the time to close my eyes and envision the event going well makes me feel better. There are many ways to incorporate visualization. Here is one that's very simple: Find a quiet place and picture yourself riding your dressage test; feel what it would be like to successfully execute all the movements. Or after you walk a jump course, imagine what riding the perfect clear round would feel like. This primes the brain and body for success. While visualization does not replace the diligence of hard work, when used in conjunction with actual practice, it can effectively rewire the brain to believe that success is achievable.

Visualization, mindfulness, and meditation are ways to get in touch with your more intuitive side. They are simple; however, do not let that trick you into thinking they are easy. Like anything else, with practice, they get better, so carve out the time.

Prioritizing Rest and Recovery

Rest and recovery can be easily overlooked; however, finding the time to work it into your daily life will pay you back tenfold. Even though I have a firm grasp of the benefits of rest and recovery for our bodies, minds, and overall well-being, and the costs of neglecting them, I still struggle to find time for this important aspect of rider fitness myself. But I never regret it when I make rest and recovery a priority. I recognize that it often takes a little extra effort to consistently find time for recharging, but with a little planning and willpower, I know you can do it. And I'm here to help! For starters, remember that this program is already a huge time-saver because it's built on the concept that you can get superior results from less work than most people anticipate. Many of my clients have been shocked to discover that working out at a high intensity for 30 minutes two or three times a week helps you progress faster and produces bigger gains than spending hours in the gym doing cardio on the elliptical or treadmill. Likewise, even short stints of meditation or visualization can yield dramatic changes for the better.

Maybe one barrier you face is that you have to clean stalls every day. If delegating this work isn't an option, try and turn chores into a time of recharging instead of stress and discomfort. You can do this by "being present" while mucking, letting your mind wander, or bringing awareness to your movements or to the task as an act of care for your horses. Focus on "staying in the moment" instead of drifting off into an endless list of the things you could be doing instead.

If we look very closely at restructuring our lives, we can often find creative solutions. And there are many small things you can do to prevent yourself from hitting a wall with your riding and training and ensuring you set aside times for rest and recovery. Write them down and treat them like any other appointment or obligation. Respect them as an equally high priority.

CHAPTER 5

Setting Yourself Up for Success

Now that we've talked about each of the four pillars of a successful rider fitness program, it's time to put the pieces together and get moving! I've worked with many busy equestrians (and I am one myself), and I know that building a program that is not overly time-consuming and that works around your riding commitments is of the utmost importance. It's taken me years to develop the program that I'm sharing with you in this book. So I am certain that with the modularity and variety of the routines, along with the detailed guidelines and scheduling tips I provide in the following pages, you can find the time and motivation to create a custom program that will help you get fitter than you've ever been before and propel your performance in the saddle to new heights. As I've said many times in this book already, you can get an awful lot out of a 30-minute workout, and when you start adding these workouts together over consecutive days, weeks, and months, you will see some startling results.

Consistency is the key to success with any exercise program. You have to do the work day in and day out (with one day off per week, of course!). There are some days that will be harder than others, but you need to find the resolve to keep going. Results come from giving consistent effort on a regular basis. Exercising inconsistently in spurts will not get you where you want to go, and at worst, could lead to injury that will set you back. You would not bring your horse to a show without doing consistent, disciplined conditioning work to get him ready. The time has come to take responsibility for your health with the same level of commitment and care you give to your horse.

Program Building Blocks

Real, lasting rider fitness is built over months of consistent exercise; however, breaking it down into obtainable weekly goals is the best place to start. This will also help you stay motivated over the long haul. Each week should consist of a balance of aerobic activity (or riding), high-intensity strength training, stretching, and rest and recovery. It will help to create a schedule to keep yourself on track. Here's what I recommend:

Five sessions of aerobic activity: At least five days a week, you should be doing aerobic activity. If you aren't riding your horse, choose another form of low-impact cardio (walking, biking, or swimming, for example). Sessions should be between 30 and 60 minutes long. If you ride multiple horses per day, you can count each session of 30 minutes or more toward your five sessions per week. It's okay to do more than five sessions, but make sure these don't cut into your time for the other three pillars of rider fitness.

Two sessions of strength training: Two times a week you should be doing the high-intensity strength training routines provided in this book. If you're new to strength training, start with sessions of about 20 minutes and work up to 30 minutes, but no more. Make sure you have at least 24 hours of rest in between strength-training sessions, and do not strength train the day before a competition. Ideally, if you plan to do a strength-training session and a cardio session on the same day, plan for a day when your riding (or other aerobic activity) will be on the lighter side so you don't overdo it and wear yourself out.

Two sessions of stretching: You should be stretching two times a week for 20 to 30 minutes at a time. Stretching time should not exceed 30 minutes.

One day of rest and recovery: One day a week should be dedicated to rest and recovery. Seriously—it's important, so don't skip it!

You might notice that this math adds up to more than seven days, so you will have to overlap workouts on some days. You could do strength training in the morning before you ride or fit in a session afterward. It might even be possible to fit all three categories of exercise into a day: You could ride first thing in the morning, do your strength training routine in the afternoon after work, and stretch before you go to bed. The way you build your program should be very specific to you. Just remember to reserve stretching for after other types of exercise so you don't overtax your muscles before you really need them.

Through trial and error, you will need to develop a schedule that works for you. This will take time so be patient with yourself. Consistency is the most important part of this program. The key is to keep working out...even when you don't feel like working out. But it's a balancing act—you also want to avoid doing too much. Think of it like preparing your horse for a dressage test: You don't want to over-drill the movements or the full test. You have to put together a program that leads to success without leading to injury. That is where timing comes in, as you do not want to overload a program with too much intensity, in sessions that are too close together. You also do not want to be doing exercises that could lead to injury.

When you are trying to figure out if what your body needs is rest and recovery or another workout, think back to the last time you did a strength-training session. If

WHEN IS THE BEST TIME OF DAY TO WORK OUT?

This is a question that I get quite often. The answer is that it varies for everyone. Some people tend to have their best workouts first thing in the morning; for others, exercising early makes them lethargic for the rest of the day. Some people love to exercise before going to bed at night, while this leaves others feeling too wired to sleep. (Remember, it's especially important not to interfere with your sleep, so if exercise pumps you up and makes you antsy, pick a different time of day.)

Personally, I know that 2:00 pm is the best time for me to work out. Any earlier and I'm tired for the rest of the day. But if I leave it for the end of the day, I will most likely blow it off. The trick is to try different times of day until you find one that doesn't make it easy to skip or leave you feeling crappy afterward. Once you've found the sweet spot, stick with it. Consistency is the ticket to success in any exercise program.

it was more than three days ago, the answer is you probably need to exercise. If it was fewer than three days ago, you probably need rest and recovery.

Schedule Your Fitness Program Around Your Horses

Since our fitness goals are all about making the most of our time in the tack, it makes sense to plan your workouts around your horse(s). Let's be honest, an exercise program won't succeed any other way! Whether you are working 10 horses a day or one horse on the weekend, riding is the top priority, and it should stay that way. I will never ask you to compromise on time with your horse; this comes first when you sit down to plan your workout schedule.

Whether you are working 10 horses a day or one horse on the weekend, riding is the top priority, and it should stay that way.

I recommend planning out a month at a time so you have a sense of the big picture. I like to print out a blank month calendar and begin with the most important (often non-negotiable) dates: my riding commitments. Write down your competition days—these are written in stone. Then mark down lesson days when your rides will be more intense, and all other riding plans, along with what type of riding you will be doing each time. Remember that riding counts toward your five weekly cardio sessions.

Next, pick one day a week that you will isolate for rest and recovery. This is not something that you fit in "if you can"; it is a highlighted and underscored *must do*. (I see you rolling your eyes—especially you, you busy professional riders—but do it anyway! I promise you won't regret it.)

Now select the days when you want to do your strength training routines. Ideally, these should be scheduled for the days when you are doing lighter rides or no cardio at all. Try to avoid scheduling two high-intensity activities back-to-back as this will quickly lead to exhaustion, burnout, lack of focus, overtraining, or injury. Record specific times for your strength-training routines and remember not to schedule two high-intensity sessions within 24 hours of each other.

Stretching can usually be squeezed into days that are already occupied with other activities, so schedule these sessions last. I find stretching before bed as part of my wind-down routine to work well, but you can also stretch after really intense cardio or strength-building sessions.

Pick a Routine and Stick with It

The strength-building routines in Part 2 are designed to be full-body workouts that you can do anywhere. To maximize the benefits of this program—to improve your overall fitness and become a more effective rider—I recommend choosing one routine and sticking with it for at least a month. As you get better at the routine and perfect each of the exercises in it, your body will begin to adapt. Correct form is what makes the exercises challenging, and your form will get better with time and consistency. Changing things up more frequently will produce inferior results.

The routines in this book are all written at a similar intensity level. The full-body routines are written to incorporate the exercises you need to improve your riding. They target the weaknesses of a rider and are written to strength your body in a well-rounded way. You can start with Routine 1 (p. 56), and after doing it for a month, move on to Routine 2 (p. 66), and so on. But you can also just select a routine that seems appealing to you because they are all written to be accessible. The upper- and lower-body routines are especially effective if you are dealing with an injury in one part of your body but still want to work out. (Which you should!)

One thing to keep in mind is something I mentioned earlier in the book: Although you won't be changing routines in a given month, you will need to keep making the routine you've selected more and more challenging by increasing the number of repetitions or the amount of time you spend on each exercise. If the routine is recommending that the exercise is done for two minutes but you can only do it for 30 seconds before becoming exhausted, that is okay. Work up to the two minutes, even if you do it five seconds at time. Some days will be harder than others. That is okay also. It is part of the process so *stick with it*. Sometimes mastering a routine will take more than a month. Don't give up or become discouraged. Everyone is different and figuring out the right pace and intensity level for your body is all part of the learning process. Building muscle memory through repetition is the key to success. With time, consistency, and a gradual increase in intensity, your body will get stronger and more adept at the exercises—even the ones that you find challenging in the beginning. That's why we focus on mastering a single routine first. As you increase the amount of time you spend on particular exercises within a routine, make sure that your high-intensity workout doesn't exceed 30 minutes overall. After 30 minutes, research shows that you experience diminishing returns on your efforts.

Once you have mastered your first routine, you can move on to another. You will know you have mastered a routine when you can do the exercises for the full amount of time assigned, and you do not feel "tested" anymore. Tackling another routine ensures you continue to challenge your body in new ways. With every new routine you begin, focus on executing each exercise with perfect form and on targeting the correct muscle groups.

Typically, it takes about six weeks to really start noticing an improvement in strength from an exercise routine. When you first begin, changes will be more about neural adaptation of learning a new movement pattern. So give yourself time to start noticing a difference in your riding. However, once you start to see improvement, you will continue to notice benefits as you continue incorporating exercise in your life. Maybe your sitting trot is more plugged in. You might be able to hold the galloping position for longer without getting tired. Maybe aches and pains that you had accepted as part of life begin to lessen or even go away.

A QUICK NOTE ABOUT YIN STRETCHES

The yin pose stretches are different from the other pillars. From the beginning you should be able to do them for the full three-minute hold (when indicated). They are stretches that target the fascia and enable it to be healthier and more pliable. Sometimes these changes are very noticeable; other times, they are more subtle. They offer a good opportunities to focus on your breathing and use the poses as practice "being present" with the sensations you feel.

Time Management

There are only 24 hours in a day, seven days in a week, and 365 (or 366) days in a year. You can't change the facts; all you can change is how effectively you use the time you have. Be conscientious about what you do each day. Check your monthly schedule every night to see what the next day will bring. And make adjustments as you go when you find a hole or something that isn't working well.

Time is your most valuable asset—you don't want to waste it. Although investing in your health can't add minutes to the day, it will improve how you feel on and off your horse—and that has a dramatic impact on the overall quality of your life.

I want to put in one last plug for the importance of rest and recovery at this point. Fight the urge to think of rest and recovery as a waste of time and think of it instead as a way of respecting your body and its essential needs. And remember, it isn't just about taking a break to unwind or using precious minutes to decompress. Rest and recovery is a necessary component of building muscle. Muscle fibers do not actually grow during exercise—they break down. It is during sleep, rest, and recovery that the fibers in your muscles lay down stronger, thicker filaments. Your body is not designed to be going, going, going all the time, and while I do want you to prioritize exercise in how you manage your time, it is just as important to schedule rest and recovery.

Special Considerations

In planning your workouts and managing your time, there are sometimes other factors that will impact your fitness regimen. Let's touch on a few of them.

Pregnancy

Pregnancy is such an exciting and nerve-racking part of a woman's life. There is no denying that it will impact your riding as your body adapts and changes to the challenges of becoming a mother. While most doctors and literature on the subject will tell you not to ride while you are pregnant, if you are healthy and your pregnancy is progressing normally, you can certainly continue to exercise. You may need to make some modifications for your changing body, and that's what a pregnancy-specific routine, like the one I provide on p. 104, is designed to help you do.

There are some exercises that are very safe to do while you're pregnant, such as the ones I've included in Routine 6 (see p. 104). There are also some things you should avoid doing, such as deep twists, exercises on your stomach, and after your fourth month, exercises that have you on your back for extended periods of time. Be aware that expectant mothers often tire sooner, so don't push yourself too hard as exhaustion leads to an increased risk of injury. The last thing you want from your exercise program is an injury that would make life even harder while you're pregnant, so make sure you listen to your body and back off when it tells you to.

I developed the strength-building routine included in this book after working with riding clients who wanted to stay active during their pregnancies. Pregnant women are some of my favorite to work with because it is such an exciting period in their lives. They know that they need to work hard and take care of their bodies. Some days are harder than others, but they always show up and give it everything they have. As a personal trainer, I could not ask for more.

There are a couple of additional exercises to use during pregnancy I want to share with you as well. They're client favorites that you can use anytime you want to get your body moving, are feeling stiff, or need a warm-up before your chosen form of low-impact cardio. The first is great for working your pelvic floor. It is important to work your pelvic floor when you are pregnant because this area "holds in" your baby. Having a strong pelvic floor also helps with delivery. This is also a great exercise for targeting the deep muscles of the core, which often grow weaker from lack of use during pregnancy.

1 Find a comfortable seated position, either in a chair or on the floor. If you are on the floor, try sitting on a pillow or cushion as this will help with any pressure you might experience in your lower back.

2 Inhale, bringing your stomach forward and arching your lower back, and as you exhale, round your lower back. You should feel your pelvis rocking back and forth on the cushion or in the chair.

Another beneficial exercise to do regularly while you're pregnant is *barrel rolls*.

1 Find a comfortable position on all fours, hands and knees planted.

2 Smoothly bring your body to one side, then up, where you exhale and round your back.

3 Continue rolling your body to the other side, and then down, arching your back as you inhale. Make this motion as smooth as possible. Imagine that you are churning your midsection.

Injury

One of the goals of this rider fitness program is to use exercise as a tool to prevent injury from happening in the first place. But that won't always be possible. Shit happens. Injuries are an inevitable part of life, and especially a life with horses. The best thing you can do when you are injured—whether you fell from your horse or fell down the stairs—is to continue to exercise.

Undertaking a fitness program that incorporates the four pillars of riding (or other aerobic activity), strength training, stretching, and rest and recovery can do a great deal to help you heal from an injury. However, there are two types of injuries—*chronic* and *acute*—and they should be approached differently when it comes to exercise.

An acute injury is one that happens suddenly and has a clear onset, although an acute injury can often lead to a chronic issue. It is important that you consult a doctor when you are dealing with an acute injury (also with certain chronic injuries that interfere with normal activities). You may need medical treatment or physical therapy (PT) before you can begin a fitness program or to supplement your workouts. If a doctor does refer you to a physical therapist, take the advice and go—PT can get you on the path to recovery. You can discuss the exercises in this book with your physical therapist, but it's unlikely that you will have time for both. After completing physical therapy, a robust fitness program can help you stay healthy and maintain gains in flexibility and strength that you attained.

In the immediate aftermath of an acute injury, getting sufficient rest is crucial. This is where *RICE* comes into play: Rest, Ice, Compress, and Elevate. Rest allows the tissues to repair—you do not want to exacerbate the problem by getting moving too early. However, as soon as your doctor gives you clearance, it's time to get moving. Going to physical therapy is a great way to improve the outcome of acute injury. A physical therapist can safely improve range of motion and strengthen the area that is injured. This way it does not become a chronic problem.

Studies have shown that patients who continue to exercise other body parts during an acute injury will actually make more progress than those who are completely sedentary. While you may to modify your exercise program to avoid the injured area of your body, you can still do a lot to improve your overall strength and exercise areas that are not impacted. The increase in blood flow that occurs during strength training will support the recovery process. (There are routines for lower-body and upper-body injuries in Part 2, which will help you get on the road back to health—see pp. 116 and 126).

Unlike an acute injury, a chronic injury, also called an *overuse injury*, develops slowly and lasts a long time. If not addressed, a chronic injury will lead to a lifetime of pain and inflammation. Chronic injuries will not go away or stay away unless you are care for them proactively. The discomfort is real, but the pain will only get worse if the surrounding muscles are allowed to atrophy. So don't ignore a chronic injury or just try to avoid using the affected area. Treating a chronic injury is a balancing act: You have to apply enough stimulus through exercise to create change, but not so much that you exacerbate the problem. Rest and recovery is a very important part of the process because this is where the body gets the opportunity to repair.

You can safely work the lower body without hurting or overusing the upper body and vice versa.

The period of rest required to recover from an injury is shorter than most people think. However, riders are a tough, stubborn bunch, and too often, I see them moving around and getting back in the saddle before their bodies have had sufficient time to heal. That's why it's important to see a doctor immediately after an acute injury, even if you don't think you need to. Shrugging off pain as part of the deal with horses is gambling with your health—that thing you think is just a sprain or a bruise could be a broken bone, and severe injuries left untended may not heal correctly. Not taking the right measures to care for an injury, or ignoring your doctor's advice and getting back to normal activity levels too soon, is how acute injuries turn into chronic (and sometimes career-ending) problems.

Upper-Body Injury

While injury can be a crushing blow to your ego and one heck of a good excuse to forget the exercise program, don't fall into this trap. You can safely work the lower body without hurting or overusing the upper body and vice versa. Doing so will help hasten the healing process and make you feel better, physically and mentally. There is so much you can still do as long as you're careful not to affect the injured area. For this reason, it's a good idea to skip exercises that require balance to eliminate the possibility of needing to catch yourself with the area of the body that is injured. The most important thing is to stay busy and keep moving. Muscle loss and atrophy are not your friends.

By necessity, you will become somewhat asymmetrical while coping with and working around an acute injury to the upper body. But the imbalance can be addressed once you've recovered. It's much more beneficial to modify your fitness program so you can stay in shape than to neglect the healthy parts of your body while an injury heals. (I provide a routine specific to those with an upper-body injury on p. 126.)

Lower-Body Injury

There is no denying that a lower-body injury can be detrimental to your overall health. Acute injury to the lower body can take a very long time to heal because the bones are bigger and they often require surgery, which usually comes with a lengthy recovery process. The biggest muscle groups are in the lower body, so lower-body injuries also tend to impact your overall fitness more than an upper-body injury will. That said, it is still important to remain active in the upper body while you recuperate from a lower-body injury. Exercises that target the upper body will help you recover faster and will keep the rest of your body fit.

In this scenario, it is probably worth investing in some hand weights so that you can optimize your exercise program for limited mobility. The weights don't need to be big—3- and 5-pound weights are quite versatile. Exercises that isolate the upper body will help keep you active while you're recovering and will increase the strength in your arms and your core.

Core exercises are particularly important because your core is activated all the time—when you ride, walk, sit down, or stand up. The "core" that we all talk about is shaped like a cylinder: the base is the pelvic floor and the top is the diaphragm—a large dome-shaped muscle at the base of the lungs. The sides of the cylinder are made up of the *transversus abdominis*, the *erector spinae*, and the *obliques*. There are many other muscle groups that make up the core, but these are the big ones. It's important to keep working as many of these muscles as possible during recovery because a strong and effective core enables you to connect with your horse. It's also needed for most movements, large and small. Note that an overly tight core can actually be a detriment to your ability to engage the horse's back by causing a blocking sensation.

The good news is that there are many

lower-body exercises that do not require the legs to bear any weight.

Illness

Exercising regularly is good for your immune system and can actually increase your white blood cells—the body's first line of defense for fighting off disease. A consistent exercise routine can also reduce the chance of getting a cold, flu, or other viruses by flushing bacteria out of the lungs and airways. However, *if you are already starting to feel sick*, it is best to avoid high-intensity exercise. This is not the time to push yourself to your limits. Rigorous exercise depletes you by placing additional stress on your immune system, which is already working hard to fend off a cold or virus. High-intensity strength training when you're under the weather can actually extend an illness, so I recommend skipping it until you feel better. What your body needs most when you are sick is extra rest and recovery.

What can you do while you're sick? If you feel up to it, continue to do your barn chores and even some light riding or other cardio. (Be aware that you could be contagious so it's a good idea to keep your distance from other people.) You can also continue to do your stretches. In fact, the yin poses are a really good, low-impact way to move lymphatic buildups.

When can you resume your workouts? You don't have to feel 100 percent to start your regular exercise program again, you just have to be feeling better. You should also make sure that you've been fever free for at least 24 hours. Getting sick is never fun and being forced to take a step back from exercise, especially when you feel like you are finally gaining momentum, can be frustrating. However, taking it slow as you come back after an illness is what you need to do if you don't want to make yourself sicker or extend the amount of time you're down and out.

Depression and Anxiety

We've touched on how exercise can help alleviate anxiety already in this book. Research overwhelmingly shows that one of the best things you can do when you are struggling mentally is to move your body. It gives you the opportunity to clear your head. When I was hospitalized for bipolar disorder, one of the best days I had in the hospital was the day I got to go to the gym. While I do not remember the exercises I did, I do remember that the act of moving my body really got me out of my own way. I felt that it gave me the ability to breathe again.

Tailoring your exercise program to your mental state is important—depression and anxiety, for instance, should be approached a little differently. When you are depressed, it's probably not the time to go all out. Setting an achievable goal like taking a walk for a half-hour and showering afterward can lead to a wonderful sense of release and accomplishment. If you can, get out and ride a horse, but try and take the pressure out of the situation as much as possible. Go on a hack with a friend or ride the old schoolmaster at the farm. Find activities that get you out of your head and into your body. Do anything that gets you moving in an enjoyable way.

Conversely, if you are dealing with anxiety, a hard workout can be just the reboot you need to stop worrying and turn your mood around. When you're in an anxious state, your body reacts as if it is facing a serious threat, causing your heart to race and your mind to swirl. A high-intensity workout that gets your heart rate up and releases endorphins will trick the body into believing you have outrun the threat.

Exercise is a powerful tool for combatting negative emotions. So let's get started.

Dealing with Setbacks

Setbacks are to be expected in anything you do. They are just a part of reality. I got my degree in exercise science. My body feels like crap when I do not work out regularly. That being said, I have gone months in my adult life without exercising. The hard part is always starting again. Usually what gets me going is pain. When I recognize that the pain I feel is from skipping a week of exercise, you will find me hitting my mat that day.

The fact is, we have busy weeks at work. We fall off and get injured. We have babies who need us every waking minute. We go on vacation and do not think once about exercising while we are there. Sometimes we fall off the exercise train for no reason at all. It is all okay. We are human. It happens. The thing is to recognize the pattern and get back on the metaphorical horse as soon as we can.

You are not perfect, and these exercise routines do not expect you to be. What I ask is that you keep trying. If you stop for more than two weeks, maybe the answer is to pick up where you left off…or you can try a completely different routine. The trick is to *get moving again*. You are strong and you got this. I believe in you.

PART 2

8 RIDER EXERCISE ROUTINES

Select one of the following routines to begin your training. As mentioned earlier in this book, I recommend sticking with the same routine for at least a month to six weeks, until you perfect each exercise and are ready to move on to new challenges. Be sure to read chapter X (Building Your Rider Fitness Program—p. 42) for more details on choosing a routine and executing the movements for maximum benefit.

These routines are designed to be practiced at home or your barn (or anywhere) with minimal equipment. No weights are required—you use your own body weight to create resistance to strengthen your muscles—but a yoga mat might make floor exercises, and especially the yin stretches (p. 148), more comfortable. (I will note when a chair or another prop is required for a particular exercise.) Have a timer on hand for exercises that need to be done for a certain duration. In some cases, you won't be able to do the prescribed number of repetitions or continue an exercise for the suggested duration—that's okay. Do what you can to start and build up to the recommended number of minutes or repetitions. Remember: it's the increase in intensity over time that will make you stronger, so it's not important where you begin.

ROUTINE 1 FULL BODY

Time Required: 20-30 minutes

Equipment Required: Yoga mat; stopwatch or phone timer

Intensity Level: 7 RPE

Routine Benefits: Improved coordination and strength in legs, core, and upper body. This routine gets your heart rate up quickly. You are working muscles in your legs that you didn't know existed. This is a great exercise routine to start with because it is challenging but not overwhelming. By the end you should feel exhausted…but like you have a little bit still left in the tank.

Jumping Jacks

1. Stand with your feet together and your arms down by your sides.
2. In one jump raise your hands out to the sides and then overhead, and spread your legs out just wider than your shoulders (Photo 1).
3. Jump back to the starting position.
4. Repeat for two minutes or as long as you can.

Curtsy Squat

1. Stand at the back end of your mat, if you're using one, slightly to the right side, with your hands at your sides. You should leave enough room in front of you to step forward.
2. Step forward with your right leg and cross your right leg over your left leg so your left leg is stretching back (Photo 1).
3. Keeping your chest tall, bend your knees so that you are in a curtsy position. Try to bring your left knee as close to the ground as you can (Photo 2).
4. Step back to starting position.
5. Repeat on the same leg 30 times or as many as you can.
6. Switch positions and cross your left leg over your right leg, doing the Curtsy Squat on that side 30 times or as many as you can.

1

2

Lunge

1. Stand tall at the front of your mat with your arms hanging at your sides and your feet hip-distance apart (Photo 1).
2. Step way back with your left leg so you can only keep your left toes on the ground. At the same time, bring your hands to the ground with your elbows locked on either side of your right leg (Photo 2).
3. Maintain a straight line from your left heel to your left shoulder.

1

4. Press the ball of your right foot to the floor and contract your left thigh muscles, pressing "up" with them to maintain your left leg in a straight position.
5. Hold for five seconds.
6. Slowly return to standing position.
7. Repeat on the other side, bringing your right leg back as you come down into a lunge position.
8. Complete 30 repetitions on each side.

2

Quadruped/Bird Dog

1. Start on all fours in a tabletop position, with your arms straight, your hands under your shoulders, and your knees under your hips (Photo 1).

2. Simultaneously extend your right arm straight forward and your left leg straight back in opposite directions. Keep your gaze and your chin down and your back flat. If you feel an arch, chances are you're lifting your leg or arm too high (Photo 2).

3. Flex your left foot so that your toes are pointing toward the ground.

1

4. Keep your core muscles tight and hold for five seconds.
5. Return to tabletop position.
6. Then extend your left arm straight forward and your right leg straight back and hold for five seconds.
7. Repeat this exercise for two minutes, alternating between right and left.

1

2

Side Lying Adduction

1. Lie down on your right side with your legs stretched out long and pressed together, your head supported by your right hand, and your left arm resting flat on your left side (Photo 1).
2. Bend your left leg and cross it over your right leg. Place your left foot on the ground just above your right knee (Photo 2).
3. Bend your left arm and place your left hand on your left hip. With control, lift your right leg off the ground with your toes pointing forward.
4. Slowly lower the right leg to the ground.
5. Repeat for 90 seconds lying on your right side then switch to the left.

3

Tricep Dips

1. Sit on the floor with your knees bent and your feet in front of you, resting on your heels.
2. Place your hands behind you, under your shoulders, with your fingers facing toward your body and your elbows bent (Photo 1).
3. Straighten your arms to lift your butt off the ground (Photo 2).
4. Lower yourself back down slowly and with control.
5. Complete 30 repetitions.

V-Up

1. Lie on your back with your arms stretched straight over your head and your legs stretched long (Photo 1).
2. Slowly and with control, use your strength rather than momentum to lift your legs and your upper body off the floor at the same time. Bring your arms over your head and reach them forward. Your legs should come to a 45-degree angle with the floor so that your torso and your legs create a "V" (Photo 2).
3. Slowly and with control, keeping your core engaged, reach your arms back over your head and lower them and your legs back down to the floor and into your starting position.
4. Complete 30 repetitions.

1

2

Lizard Pose Stretch
(Three-Minute Hold)

1. Stand at the front of your mat with your hands by your sides (Photo 1).
2. Step back with your right leg into your forward lunge position.
3. Place both hands flat on the ground to the right of your left (bent) leg, keeping your arms straight (Photo 2).
4. Hold for three minutes, remembering to breathe.
5. Slowly switch positions so your left leg is stretched back and your right leg is bent, and repeat the stretch.
6. *For added challenge:* If you have the flexibility to do this without pain, bend your arms and bent knee until you are all the way down on your forearms. It's also fine to ride it high as shown here, staying on your hands with your arms straight. This stretch is great for targeting the hip flexors. It should get easier over time, but if you feel sharp pain at any point, come out of the stretch carefully and slowly. Don't push yourself to the point of injury.

ROUTINE

2 FULL BODY

Time Required: 20-30 minutes

Equipment Required: Yoga mat; stopwatch or phone timer

Intensity Level: RPE 8

Benefits: This is a program for targeting core strength. You work the rest of the body, but your center will have to embrace the burn.

Alternating Sit-Up

1. Sit on your butt with your knees bent and your feet flat on the floor.
2. Lower your upper body down to the mat, leaving your knees bent. Place both hands behind your head (Photo 1).
3. Sit up "crunch" style, bringing your right elbow toward your left knee while leaving your left shoulder on the ground. Engage your core muscles (Photo 2).
4. Lower yourself back down on the mat.
5. Do the same thing on the other side: Sit up, bringing your left elbow toward your right knee, leaving your right shoulder on the ground.
6. Lower yourself back down to the mat.
7. Repeat for two minutes, continuing to alternate sides. When you do this exercise correctly, you should feel it in your *obliques*—the muscles on each side of your torso.

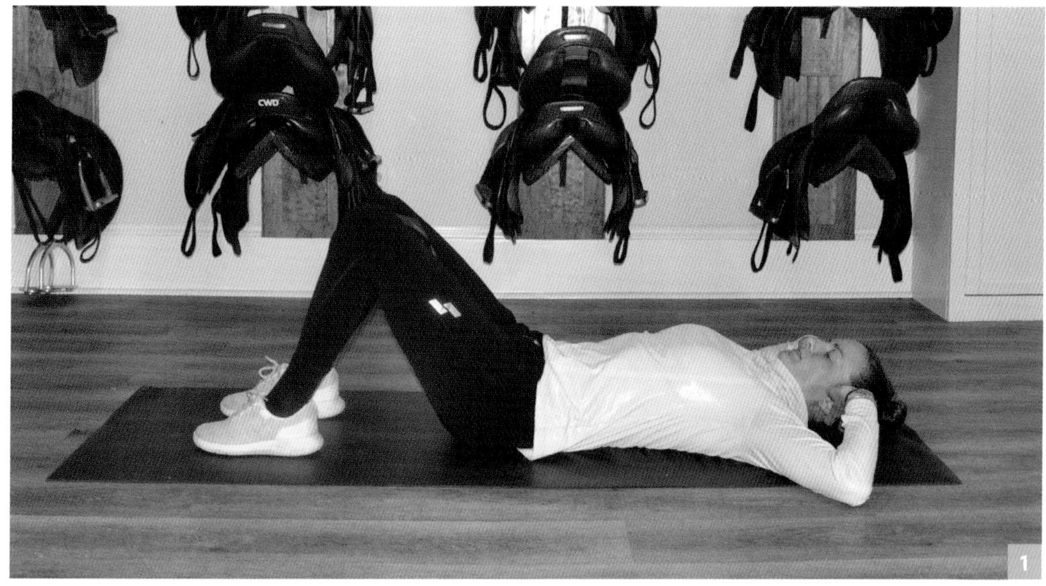
CWD
1

CWD
2

Bridge with Leg Lifts

1. Lie on your back with your knees bent, feet flat on the floor, and heels directly under your knees. Your arms should be straight by your sides with the palms down.

2. Squeeze in your core and your glutes and push your hips up toward the ceiling (Photo 1).

1

3. Keeping your hips level, lift one leg off the floor with the knee still bent, like you are marching while lying on your back. Then return that leg to your start position (Photo 2).
4. Lift your other leg off the floor in the same way, keeping your hips level. Then bring that leg back down.
5. Repeat for two minutes, alternating sides. Note that people tend to want to hold their breath during this exercise, so remember to keep breathing.

Clamshell

1. Lie on your left side with your left arm bent and supporting your head. Bend your knees up toward your chest with your feet together (Photo 1).
2. Keeping your core engaged, slowly and with control, "open" your right knee away from your left, as high as you can get it (Photo 2). Try to isolate the movement to your leg, keeping your back flat and still. Do not rotate through your lumbar spine.
3. Slowly lower your knee back down.
4. Repeat for two minutes, then switch to your right side and repeat for two minutes.

1

2

Reverse Lunge with Lateral Extension

1. Stand at the front of your mat with your feet together and arms by your sides (Photo 1).
2. Step back with your right foot so only your right toes are making contact and your left leg is bent with your thigh parallel to the floor. Simultaneously raise your arms out to the sides, stopping at shoulder height (Photo 2).
3. Step forward and drop your arms.
4. Repeat with the right leg for two minutes.
5. Switch sides, stepping back with your left leg while simultaneously lifting your arms out to the sides. Repeat for two minutes.

1

2

Lateral Low Lunge

1. Face the long side of your mat. Stand up straight with your feet shoulder-width apart and your hands on your hips.
2. Step out to the left, squatting down on your left leg with your feet flat on the floor and your right leg extended. Go low enough to feel the muscles work.
3. Squeeze your glutes and press off your left foot to return to the starting position.
4. Repeat on the left side for one minute.
5. Switch to the right side and repeat the same movement for one minute.

Body Saw

1

1. Begin face down on your mat on your forearms and toes with your body straight and level in a plank position. Your elbows should be under your shoulders. Make fists with your hands and keep your gaze down so your neck is in line with your spine (Photo 1).
2. Keeping your body straight and level and engaging your core, rock your whole body forward so just the tips of your toes stay in contact (Photo 2).
3. Rock your whole body back to your starting position.
4. Repeat for two minutes.

2

Superman

1. Lie on your stomach with your legs stretched out behind you, toes pointed. Place your hands under your shoulders with your elbows bent and press your forehead to the ground (Photo 1).
2. Engage through your core and squeeze your glutes to lift your upper body, arms, and legs off the ground. Point your toes and keep your legs straight as you stretch your arms out to the sides (like Superman!). Tuck your chin slightly and keep your gaze down (Photo 2).
3. Hold for three seconds. Then return with control to your starting position. (Try not to collapse in a pile on the floor.)
4. Repeat for two minutes.

Butterfly
(Three-Minute Hold)

1. Sit on your butt. Bring the soles of your feet together in front of you. Sit up tall, looking straight ahead and grasping your toes with your hands, keeping your arms straight (Photo 1).
2. Fold forward over your legs, keeping your hands around your toes as you bend your arms and lower your head. Hold for three minutes. (Note: The closer your feet are to your body, the more you will feel this stretch in your inner thighs. The farther your feet are from your body, the more you will feel this stretch in your lower back.)

1

2

ROUTINE

3 FULL BODY

Time Required: 20-30 minutes

Equipment Required: Yoga mat

Intensity Level: RPE 7

Benefits: This is a great routine for improving knee stability, as it works the muscles that stabilize and support the knees. It is also great for the core.

Narrow-Leg Squat

1. Stand with your feet shoulder-width apart, toes straight ahead, and arms hanging at your sides (Photo 1).

1

2. Keeping your back straight and your hands on your hips, bend at your knees and hips at the same time. Push your butt back and down, and lower yourself with control into a squat position (Photo 2).
3. Go as low as you can without resting at the bottom. Ideally, your heels should stay on the ground.
4. Keep the weight evenly distributed in your feet as you slowly push back up to standing.
5. Repeat for two minutes.

2

1

2

Wide-Leg Squat

1. Stand with your feet apart, wider than your shoulders, and your hands on your hips, facing the long side of your mat. Your toes should be pointed out slightly (Photo 1).
2. Keeping your back straight, bend at the knees and hips at the same time. Pushing your butt back and down, lower yourself with control into a wider-legged version of the Narrow-Leg Squat you just did (Photo 2).
3. Go as low as you can. Ideally, your heels should stay on the ground.
4. Without resting at the bottom, keep the weight evenly distributed in your feet, and slowly push back up to your starting position.
5. Repeat for two minutes.

Knee Push-Up

1. Start on your hands and knees. Walk your hands forward and plant them a little wider than shoulder width-apart, so just on the outside edges of your mat (Photo 1).
2. Maintaining a straight line from ears to hips to knees, lower yourself down as slowly as you can, trying to touch your nose to the ground (Photo 2).
3. Push yourself back up as slowly as you can, keeping an even pressure in both hands.
4. Do three sets of 25 repetitions.

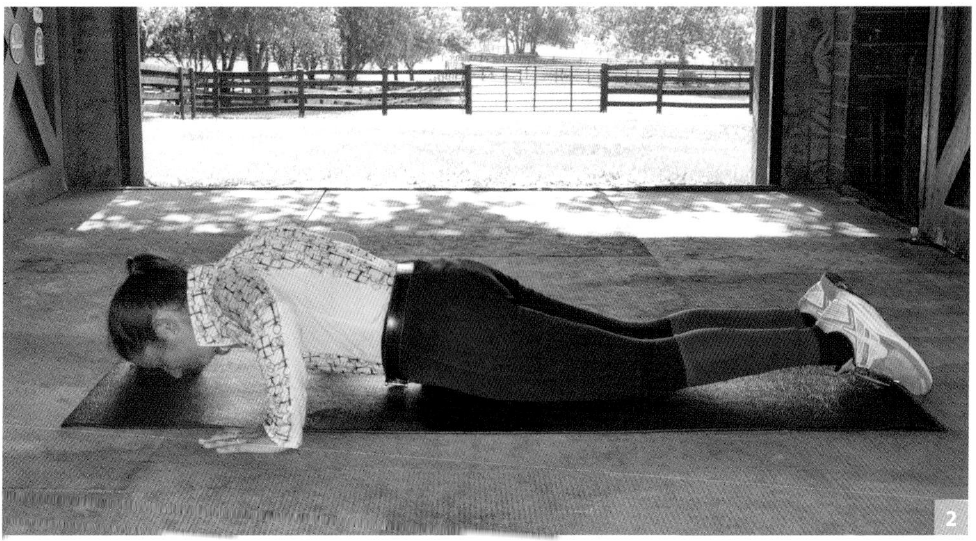

Fire Hydrants

1. Start on your hands and knees, with your hands under your shoulders and your knees under your hips (Photo 1).

2. Engaging through your core and keeping your hips square and your back straight and flat, lift your left leg out to the side with your knee bent (Photo 2).
3. Hold for one second.
4. Lower the leg in toward your body and pause with your knee hovering above the ground.
5. Repeat for two minutes on each side.

Scissor Kicks

1. Lie on your back with your arms at your sides and your lower back pushed into the floor.
2. Lift your legs off the ground and hold them straight up toward the ceiling. Keep your toes flexed toward the floor (Photo 1).
3. Lower one leg straight in front of you until it's about 6 inches above the ground, bring it back up, and then do the same with the other leg (Photos 2 & 3).
4. Continue alternating lowering your legs for two minutes.

1

2

3

Bridge

1. Lie on your back with your knees bent, your feet flat to the floor, and your heels under your knees. Rest your arms by your sides with your palms facing down (Photo 1).
2. Engaging your core, push your belly button up toward the ceiling. Squeeze your glutes and your quads and hold for 30 seconds (Photo 2).
3. Lower back down to ground.
4. Hold your bridge for 30 seconds three times.

1

2

Bicycle Crunch

1. Lie on your back with your hands behind your head, your knees bent, and your feet flat on the ground.
2. Engage through your core and rotate through your torso, bringing your left elbow toward your right knee as you straighten your left leg and lift it off the ground (Photo 1).
3. Switch to the other side, bringing your right elbow toward your left knee and lifting and straightening your right leg.
4. Repeat for two minutes, continuing to alternate sides. Once you get going, your legs will both hover above the ground, rather than touching down between reps.

1

2

1

2

Tricep Dips

1. Sit on the floor with your knees bent and your feet in front of you, resting on your heels.
2. Place your hands behind you under your shoulders with your fingers facing toward your body and your elbows bent (Photo 1).
3. Straighten your arms to slowly lift your butt off the ground.
4. Lower yourself back down slowly and with control.
5. Repeat for two minutes.

Frog Stretch
(Three-Minute Hold)

1. Get on all fours.

2. Bring your feet together and your knees out as wide as you can as you fold forward and slide your arms straight out in front of you with your palms down (Photo 1).

3. Lower your hips toward your heels and try to relax as much as possible into the position.

4. Hold as still as you can for three minutes. This stretch is great for targeting the inner thighs and hips—areas we tend to ask a lot of in the saddle.

FULL BODY

Time Required: 20-30 minutes

Equipment Required: Yoga mat; stopwatch or phone timer

Intensity Level: RPE 9

Benefits: This routine is good for strengthening across your chest and your arms, as well as strengthening your core and your quads.

Bridge with Arm Lift

1. Lie on your back and bring your heels under your knees with your feet flat to the floor. Your arms should be relaxed at your sides with your palms facing down (Photo 1).
2. Engage through your core, lift your hips off the ground, and bring your arms up and over your head at the same time in one fluid motion. Your arms should land on the ground stretched straight behind your head with your palms facing up toward the ceiling (Photo 2).

3

4

5

3. Lower your hips back down, leaving your hand above your head (Photo 3).
4. Raise your hips up (Photo 4).
5. Lower your hips down to the mat as you bring your arms up over your head and back to your sides, so you are in the start position again (Photo 5).
6. Repeat for two minutes.

Cat-Cow

1. Start on all fours with your knees under your hips and your wrists lined up under your shoulders with your arms straight. Your back should be flat and your gaze down with your neck in line with your spine.

2. Lower your belly button down toward the ground. At the same time, look up, exaggerating the arch in your back. This is Cow Pose (Photo 1).

3. Bring your belly button in toward your spine and push up through both hands as you round your spine toward the ceiling. This is Cat Pose (Photo 2).

4. Repeat for two minutes, alternating fluidly between the two poses. Try synchronizing your breath so you're inhaling when you arch your back (in Cow Pose) and exhaling when you round your spine (in Cat Pose).

Downward Dog with Pawing

1. Start on all fours.
2. Straighten your legs and arms, pushing your hips up toward the ceiling so you are in a downward "V" shape (Photo 1).
3. Bend one knee, making a pawing motion with that foot (Photo 2).
4. Bend the other knee and paw with that foot (Photo 3).
5. Paw for 30 seconds, alternating legs.
6. Then find stillness with both legs straight in your starting position. Really think about trying to push your heels toward the ground. Hold for 30 seconds.
7. Do three repetitions of pawing for 30 seconds, then holding for 30 seconds.

1

2

3

Reverse Lunge with Lateral Extension

1. Stand at to the top of your mat with your feet should-width apart, shoulders back, and arms hanging at your sides. Look straight ahead (Photo 1).
2. In one fluid motion, step back with your right foot and lower your right knee toward the ground as you raise your arms straight out to the sides at shoulder height. Your left knee should be at roughly a 90-degree angle to the ground (Photo 2).
3. Step forward and bring your arms back to your sides.
4. Repeat on the same leg for one minute.
5. Then switch to stepping back with your left leg while simultaneously lifting your arms out to the side. Repeat for one minute on the left side.

1

2

Tempo Body Weight Squat

1

1. Stand at the front of your mat with your hands on your hips and step your feet out, a little wider than shoulder-width apart (Photo 1).
2. With control and keeping your back straight (do not let your lower back round), slowly lower your hips down. Keep your feet flat to the floor as you go as low as you can. Count slowly to five as you descend—this movement should be super slow. Hold at the bottom for three seconds (Photo 2).
3. Slowly and with control, count to five as you come back up to starting position.
4. Repeat for two minutes. You will feel this exercise in your quadriceps and hamstrings.

2

Push-Up

1. Position yourself in a high plank with your hands wider than shoulder-width apart, your arms straight, and your core engaged. You should be up on your toes with your legs stretched out long behind you. Imagine that there is a straight line from your ears to your ankles—like a plank of wood (Photo 1).
2. With control, lower yourself down as low as you can go, bending your elbows and keeping your back straight (Photo 2).
3. Keep your core tight and push back up.
4. Do three sets of 10 repetitions.

1

2

Plank

1. With your forearms on the ground, place your elbows directly under your shoulders and extend your legs out behind you with your toes tucked under.
2. Engage through your core, pressing up onto your toes and forearms and lifting your belly off the ground. Cast your gaze down and maintain a straight line from your neck, through your upper back, through your hips, knees, and ankles (Photo 1).
3. Hold for as long as you can. Count while you're holding, and if your first hold is shorter than 90 seconds, repeat so that you end up holding in a plank position for a total of 90 seconds.

1

2

Leg Lifts

1. Lie on your back and place your hands palm-down under your glutes to support your lower back.
2. Engage through your core and lift your neck and head off the ground as you raise your legs straight up above your hips so they are perpendicular to the ground. Flex your toes toward your body (Photo 1).
3. Slowly and with control, lower your legs down together until they are 6 inches above the ground. Never let your heels touch the ground, and keep your toes flexed back toward your body (Photo 2).
4. Raise your legs back up above your hips.
5. Repeat for two minutes.

Reclined Butterfly
(Three-Minute Hold)

1. Lie on your back and bring the soles of your feet together, letting your knees fall out wide.
2. Hold this position for three minutes.

ROUTINE

5 FULL BODY

Time Required: 20-30 minutes

Equipment Required: Yoga mat and a stopwatch

Intensity Level: RPE 7

Routine Benefits: This routine is great for strengthening your back and obliques, and also has benefits for your hips.

1

Butt Kicks

1. Start in a standing position.
2. As if you are jogging in place, kick your heels up high toward your glutes one at a time—left leg, then the right. Maintain a pace that gets your heart rate up; push yourself to go a little faster if you can (Photos 1 & 2).
3. Repeat for two minutes.

2

Twisting Knee Raise

1. Start by standing with your feet shoulder-width apart, your arms in a field-goal-post shape, and your palms facing forward (Photo 1).
2. Engage through your core and raise your right knee toward your belly button, simultaneously bringing your left elbow toward the raised knee. Try and get your knee and elbow to touch (Photo 2).
3. Return to your starting position and repeat on other side (Photo 3).
4. Continue to alternate sides for two minutes.

1

2

Front Plank

1. Sit on your butt with your knees bent and feet flat on the floor. Place your arms behind you with your hands on the floor and your fingers pointing toward your body (Photo 1).

2. Press up through your palms and raise your hips and butt off the ground, resting on your heels. Maintain a straight line with your body from your shoulders to your feet (Photo 2).

3. Hold for as long as you can, building up to 90 seconds.

4. For an extra challenge, raise one leg off the ground and hold for 30 seconds, then switch legs.

Knee-Pull Plank

1. Start in high plank position, with arms straight under your shoulders and legs extended (Photo 1).
2. Bring your right knee forward as close as you can to the center of your chest (Photo 2).
3. Keeping your spine straight, now straighten out the right leg and raise it toward the ceiling.
4. Repeat on the same side for one minute, then switch to the other leg.

1

2

Thigh Rock Back

1. Begin by kneeling on your mat with a straight back and your hands on your hips (Photo 1).
2. Lean back, keeping your body in a straight line and your core strong. Do not arch your back too much (Photo 2).
3. Flex your glute muscles and slowly return to the start position.
4. Repeat for two minutes.

Kneeling Side Kick

1. Start in a kneeling position on your mat.
2. Lean your upper body to the right and place your right hand on the floor under your shoulder. Place you left hand behind your head and stretch your left leg out to the side like a kickstand, then lift it up to the height of your hip and straighten it (Photo 1).
3. Then, keeping your left leg at hip height, kick it straight out in front of you (Photo 2).
4. Repeat on the same side for two minutes then switch sides and repeat for two minutes.

1

2

Double-Leg Ab Press

1. Lie on your back and lift your legs, bending your knees at a 90-degree angle. Your thighs should be perpendicular to the floor. Place each hand on the front of the corresponding knee (Photo 1).

2. Engaging through your core and pressing your lower back into the floor, lift your shoulders off the ground in a crunch. Keep your eyes up and your neck straight—don't tuck your chin. Create resistance by pushing your hands and knees toward each other (Photo 2).

3. Hold for 90 seconds.

Reclined Pigeon
(Three-Minute Hold, Each Side)

1. Lie on your back with your butt about 10 inches from a wall. Place your legs straight up the wall (Photo 1).
2. Cross your right leg over the left in what's called a "figure four" position (it looks like an upside down "4"). Your right ankle should be crossed just below your knee and your left foot should be flat against the wall (Photo 2).
3. Bend your left leg and slide it down the wall. Stop when you feel a nice tug at the outside of your right hip (Photo 3).
4. Hold for three minutes.
5. Switch and do the same thing with the other side. Hold for three minutes.

1

2

3

ROUTINE

6 PREGNANCY

Time Required: 20-30 minutes

Equipment Required: Yoga mat; stopwatch or phone timer; chair; 3- to 5-pound weights or cans of food (optional)

Intensity Level: RPE 5–6

Routine Benefits: I developed the strength-building routine below after working with riding clients who wanted to stay active during their pregnancies. The intent is to keep you limber and at a base level of strength as your body changes and you may become more limited in exercise options. For some parts of this routine, you have the option of adding light weights (or cans of food) to increase the intensity. You can also do these exercises without weights. You need to decide what your body can handle.

Windmills

1. Stand with your feet wider than shoulder-width apart and your arms reaching straight out to the sides, like a star (Photo 1).

2. Bend at the waist and reach for your left toe with your right hand. You do not need to touch your toe—just get as close as you can (Photo 2).

1

3. Return to your starting position (Photo 3).
4. Go the other way. Bend at the waist and reach for your right toe with your left hand.
5. Continue, alternating sides for two minutes. Move deliberately, finding the pace that is right for your body. If you feel dizzy or lightheaded, sit down.

2

3

4

Marching Crunch

1. Stand with your feet wider than shoulder-width apart and your arms in a field-goal-post shape—arms straight out from your shoulders and elbows bent at 90 degrees, palms facing forward (Photo 1).
2. Lift your left leg up, bringing your knee up as high as you can, and round your back, bringing your right elbow to your left knee (Photo 2).
3. Place your left foot down so you're back in starting position.

4. Lift your right leg up, bringing your left elbow to your right knee (Photo 3).
5. Continue alternating leg lifts from side to side like you're marching in place for one minute.
6. Take a 30-second break, then repeat for another minute.

3

Squat with Abduction

1. Stand with your feet wider than hip-width apart and place your hands under your belly (Photo 1).
2. Keeping your core strong and your chest held high, bend at the knees, lowering your butt down into a squat. Continue to support your belly (Photo 2).
3. As you stand up again, kick your left leg out to side, keeping your left knee bent (Photo 3).

4. Place your left foot down and squat again (Photo 4).

5. This time, kick out your right leg as you stand up (Photo 5).

6. Repeat 30 times on each side.

Bent-Over Fly

Equipment Note: To increase the intensity and the potential for strength-building, you can hold 3- to 5-pound weights or cans of food.

1. Stand with your feet shoulder-width apart and your knees slightly bent.
2. Bend at the waist so your upper body is at a 45-degree angle. Straighten your arms toward the ground (Photo 1).
3. Keeping your knees bent and your torso still, bring your arms straight out to the side like wings. Focus on squeezing your shoulder blades together as you do this (Photo 2).
4. Bring your arms down in front of you, back to starting position.
5. Repeat for 30 seconds, then rest for 10 seconds.
6. Repeat the entire sequence three times.

Shoulder Press

Equipment Note: To increase the intensity and the potential for strength-building, you can hold 3- to 5-pound weights or cans of food.

1. Stand with your feet shoulder-width apart and your knees slightly bent. Make a field-goal-post shape with your arms (Photo 1).
2. Keeping your core tight, push up to a standing position and push your arms up over your head until they're straight (Photo 2).
3. Return to your starting position, with knees slightly bent and goal-post arms.
4. Repeat for 30 seconds, then rest for 10 seconds.
5. Repeat the entire sequence three times.

1

2

Standing Row with Tricep Extension

Equipment Note: To increase the intensity and the potential for strength-building, you can hold 3- to 5-pound weights or cans of food.

1. Stand with your feet shoulder-width apart and your knees slightly bent. Bend at the waist so your upper body is at a 45-degree angle, and reach your arms down toward the ground (Photo 1).
2. With your thumbs up and forearms straight, pull your elbows back by your sides in a rowing motion. Squeeze your shoulder blades together while you do this (Photo 2).

1

2

3. Straighten your elbows and push your forearms back behind you to engage the tricep muscles at the back of the upper arms (Photo 3).
4. Bend your elbows back by your sides as in Step 2.
5. Bring your arms down in front of you, back to your starting position.
6. Repeat for two minutes. Move slowly and with control, and really focus on your form.

Wall Push-Up

1. Face a wall and place your hands in front of you with your arms straight at about shoulder height. Your hands should be about 4 inches wider than shoulder-width apart (Photo 1).
2. Walk your feet back so you're leaning your weight against the wall. The farther back your feet are from the wall, the more challenging the exercise will be. Slide your hands down so they are parallel to the floor.
3. Smoothly and with control, bend at the elbows and lower your whole body toward the wall. Keep your body straight. Try to get to the point where your nose is almost touching the wall (Photo 2).
4. Push yourself back up as slowly as you can.
5. Continue the push-ups for two minutes, then hold yourself in position close to the wall for 10 seconds.

Arm Stretch
(Three-Minute Hold)

1. Sit in a chair with your feet flat on the ground.
2. Sitting tall with your shoulders back, extend both of your arms straight in front of you with your palms up.
3. Grab your left fingertips with your right hand and pull your fingers down until you feel tension along your left forearm (Photo 1).
4. Remain as still as possible and hold the stretch for three minutes, then switch to the other arm.

ROUTINE 7

UPPER BODY

Time Required: 20-30 minutes

Equipment Required: Yoga mat; timing device; a chair (if using); 3- to 5-pound weights

Intensity Level: RPE 7

Benefits: This routine allows you to stay in shape rather than neglect the healthy parts of your body while an injury heals. Note most of the exercises in this routine can be performed seated in a chair or standing.

1

Arm Circles

1. Stand with your feet together and your arms straight out to the sides (Photo 1).
2. Keeping your elbows straight, circle your arms forward in circles of about a foot in diameter (Photos 2 & 3).
3. Repeat for one minute then reverse direction, doing backward arm circles for one minute.

2

3

1

Twist

1. Stand with your feet together. Bring your arms straight out to the sides, then place your fingertips on your shoulders (Photo 1).
2. Twisting at the waist, turn your whole upper body to the left, bringing your right elbow forward and your left elbow back. Think of your whole trunk as one unit (Photo 2).
3. Then switch and twist to the right (Photo 3).
4. Continue to go back and forth for two minutes.

2

3

Side Bend

1. Sit or stand with your back straight and tall and your feet together.
2. Reach your right arm overhead as you bend at the waist to the left. At the same time, reach your left arm straight down toward the ground (Photo 1).
3. Reach your left arm overhead as you bend at the waist to the right with your right arm extending straight toward the ground (Photo 2).
4. Repeat, alternating sides, for two minutes.

1

2

Tricep Extensions

1. Stand with your feet hip-width apart and your arms at your sides.
2. Lean forward so your upper body is at a 45-degree angle. Keep your elbows glued to your sides and make your hands into fists with your thumbs on top (Photo 1).
3. Straighten your arms, really focusing on contracting the muscles at the back of your upper arms.
4. Repeat for two minutes.

1

2

Shoulder Press

1. Stand with your feet hip-width apart and your arms in field-goal-post position. Make a fist with each hand (Photo 1).
2. Push your arms up over your head until they're straight (Photo 2).
3. Lower your arms back to goal-post position, and repeat for two minutes.

1

2

Elbow Press

1. Stand with your feet hip-width apart and your elbows and palms together in front of you with your fingers pointed straight up. Your elbows should be at about shoulder-height (Photo 1).
2. Keeping your elbows and palms glued together, reach straight up to the sky until your elbows are in front of your face (Photo 2).
3. Push your elbows down toward the ground, taking your arms down as far as you can with your elbows still pressed firmly together (Photo 3).
4. Repeat for two minutes. Go to the limit of your range of motion with this exercise. You may be able to lift your arms only a couple of inches, but that's fine. This a great move for working underneath the shoulder blades, no matter how far you can go.

1

2

3

Pec Press

1. Stand with your feet hip-width apart and your arms in field-goal-post position (Photo 1).
2. Keeping your elbows at shoulder height, bring your arms forward until your elbows and hands meet in the middle (Photo 2).
3. Return to goal-post position, and repeat for two minutes.

1

2

1

Elbow Pulls

1. Stand with your feet hip-width apart and your arms straight out to the sides with your palms up (Photo 1).
2. Pull your elbows into your sides, squeezing your shoulder blades together. Your palms should remain open (Photo 2).
3. Straighten your arms out again, and repeat for two minutes.

2

Broken Wing
(Three-Minute Hold)

1

1. Sit on your butt with your knees bent and your feet flat on the ground in front of you. Stretch your left arm out to the side with your hand open and your thumb pointing down toward the ground (Photo 1).

2. Bend your left elbow and reach behind you, placing the back of your hand against the small of your back. The higher up on your back your hand can reach, the more you will feel this stretch in your shoulder (Photo 2).

2

3. Lie down, keeping your left arm behind your back as you straighten your legs in front of you (Photo 3).

4. Hold for three minutes and then repeat with your right arm.

5. To make your way out of this stretch, bend your left leg if you're lying on your left arm and your right leg if you're lying on your right arm, and push yourself to the opposite side, rolling your body away and allowing you to free the arm.

3

ROUTINE

8 LOWER BODY

Time Required: 20-30 minutes

Equipment Required: Yoga mat; stopwatch or phone timer

Intensity Level: RPE 7

Benefits: Doing a lower-body-specific routine can be a great way to exercise if you have an upper-body injury. However, you can also do a lower-body routine when you are feeling sore or you just want to work on lower-body strength. Targeting the lower body will also get your heart rate up faster than an upper-body workout because you are working larger muscle groups.

Lunge

1. Stand at the front of your mat with your hands on your hips (Photo 1).
2. Step back with your right foot, keeping the toes of your right foot and your whole left foot planted on the ground (Photo 2).
3. With your shoulders over your hips, bend your right knee and lower it toward the ground, stopping with it hovering just above the ground (Photo 3).
4. Straighten your right knee, returning to the lunge back position (Photo 4)
5. Repeat lowering and raising your right knee for up to two minutes.
6. Switch sides and repeat the exercise with your left leg for up to two minutes. You will feel this in quads and in your glutes (Photo 5).

2

3

4

5

Tempo Body Weight Squat

1. Stand with your hands on your hips and step your feet out, a little wider than shoulder-width apart (Photo 1).
2. With control, keeping your back straight, lower your hips down. Keep your feet flat to the floor and go as low as you can. Do not let your lower back round. Count slowly to five as you descend—this movement should be super slow. Hold at the bottom for three seconds (Photo 2).
3. Slowly return to your starting position, again counting to five as you rise.
4. Repeat for two minutes. You will feel this exercise in your quadriceps and hamstrings.

1

2

Standing Abduction

1

1. Stand in the middle of the mat, facing one long side (Photo 1).
2. Engage through your core as you lift your left leg out to the side as high as you can while keeping your hips square over your feet. Do not lean to the side (Photo 2).
3. Hold your left leg out to the side for a count of two seconds.
4. Lower it back down to the ground.
5. Repeat for two minutes
6. Switch to raising your right leg, and repeat for two minutes. You should feel this in your hip, glutes, and core (Photo 3).

2

3

Side Lying Adduction

1. Lie on your right side with your right hand supporting your head and your left hand on your hip (Photo 1).
2. Place your left foot flat on the ground in front of you (Photo 2).
3. Lift your right leg up off the ground as high as you can, flexing your foot back toward you to keep a muscular contraction all the way down your leg (Photo 3).
4. Lower your right leg back down to the ground.

1

2

5. Repeat lifting your right leg at a slow and controlled pace of one second up and one second down. Do this for up to two minutes.
6. Switch to lying on your left side and lifting and lowering your left leg for up to two minutes. You will feel this in your inner thighs (Photos 4 & 5).

3

4

5

Straight Leg Glute Bridge

1. Start by lying on your back with knees bent and your feet flat on the ground (Photo 1).
2. Straighten your left leg (Photo 2).
3. Engage through your core and lift your glutes off the ground. Keeping your left leg straight, lift it to the height of your right knee (Photo 3).
4. Lower your body and leg back down to ground.
5. Repeat for up to two minutes on the left side.
6. Switch so your right leg is extended and your left bent (Photo 4).
7. Repeat the exercises for up to two minutes on your right side. You will feel this in your core, glutes, quads, and hamstrings (Photo 5).

1

2

3

4

5

Active Butterfly

1. Lie on your back with your feet together and knees relaxed wide (Photo 1).
2. Bring your knees together (Photo 2).
3. Slowly and with control, lower your knees back down.
4. Repeat for up to two minutes. You will feel this exercise in your inner thigh and pelvic floor.

1

2

Wide Leg Up the Wall
(Three-Minute Hold)

1. Sit as close as you can facing a wall or fence, lie back, and extend your legs straight up the wall (Photo 1).

2. Open your feet out as wide as they will comfortably go. Let gravity do the work; don't engage your muscles to pull them wider (Photo 2).

3. Hold this stretch for three minutes.

1

2

PART 3

2 YIN YOGA ROUTINES

Yin comes from the Chinese philosophical concept of Yin and Yang. One does not exist without the other, and the two forces work together. Yang represents the more active and fiery, while yin means something is more still, subtle, and cooling. As I mentioned early in the book, yin yoga is a slow-paced style of yoga as exercise with poses that are held for longer periods of time than in other styles. The yin routines are designed to tend to your connective tissue and fascia more than your muscles. Ideally, you should do them two times per week. If your body craves for you to stretch more, they are also a great way to wind down at the end of any day. (Note that I do not suggest using them to stretch before riding or exercising.)

Remain as still as possible while in them, and do not use your muscular strength to hold the poses. Try to relax into them and focus on your breath. Note, however, that you should come out of any pose that feels in some way "sharp," "electric," or hard to breathe with. Also, you may be slow-moving when you come out of these long static holds; oftentimes, we feel the pose more on the release than while doing it.

ROUTINE

1 FULL BODY

Time Required: 30 minutes
Equipment Required: Yoga mat; stopwatch or phone timer; bolster
Intensity Level: RPE 2
Benefits: This yin sequence really tends to the needs of the lower back and hips. Yin yoga soothes the body and calms the mind. Feel free to have meditative music on in the background. Remember to note when your mind wanders and return the focus to your breath.

Sphinx

1. Lie on your belly with your hands folded under your head (Photo 1).
2. Bring your elbows under your shoulders and let your belly sink into the ground. Your hands should be held together in front of you and your head should be up. Try to be as still as possible, letting go of any tension you are holding in your body (Photo 2).
3. Hold for three minutes. You should feel the stretch in your lower back. You may also start to feel it in in your shoulders and neck after a little while.

1

2

Twisted Roots

1. Lie on your back with your feet flat on the ground (Photo 1).
2. Tightly cross your right leg over your left leg so there is no gap between your legs (Photo 2).
3. Let both legs fall over to left (Photo 3).
4. Relax into this position for three minutes. If the twist is too intense, place a bolster under your legs to prop them up a little higher.

1

2

5. Switch to the other side by crossing your left leg over your right leg and letting your legs fall to the left (Photos 4 & 5).

6. Maintain the stretch for three minutes. You should feel it in your sacroiliac (SI) joint and through your thoracic spine.

3

4

5

Reclined Butterfly

1. Lie on your back with your knees bent and your feet flat on the ground (Photo 1).
2. Bring the bottoms of your feet together and let your knees fall out toward the ground (Photo 2).
3. Maintain this position as still as you can for three minutes. You should feel the stretch in your inner thigh.

1

2

Child's Pose

1. Start on your hands and knees (Photo 1).
2. Bring your feet together and your knees out wide (Photo 2).
3. Rock your hips back, stretch your arms forward, and bring your face down between your arms (Photo 3).
4. Hold this positon for three minutes. Try to let go in the areas where you feel your muscles contracting. You should sense the stretch in your hips, your lower back, and your shoulders.

1

2

3

Bolster Under Glutes

1. Lie on your back with your feet on the ground. Have a bolster within reach (Photo 1).
2. Lift your glutes up by engaging your core, and slide the bolster underneath them (Photo 2).
3. This might be plenty enough of an inversion for you. If the position feels good, stay here. If you would like more of a stretch, lift your legs straight up above your hips (Photo 3).
4. Maintain this position for a one-minute hold. You should feel it in your hips and lower back. If you choose to bring your legs up above your hips, you will likely feel a stretch in your hamstrings, as well.

Supported Fish

1. Sit on your mat with with your knees bent in front of you and one short end of the bolster close behind (Photo 1).
2. Lie back on the bolster with your arms stretched out into a T-position (Photo 2).
3. Hold for three minutes.
4. You should feel this across your chest, and maybe depending how tight the fascia is, you may feel this in your lower back.

1

2

ROUTINE

2 FULL BODY

Time Required: 30 minutes

Equipment Required: Yoga mat; stopwatch or phone timer; bolster

Intensity Level: RPE 2

Benefits: This yin sequence is great for the side-body and iliotibial (IT) band. The deep twists are said to aid in digestion. This yin sequence can be done after a long hard day to help slow the mind. I find it is a great way to unwind before bed.

Banana

1. Lie flat on your back with your legs out straight in front of you and your arms by your sides (Photo 1).
2. Bring your feet together to the lower left corner of the mat (Photo 2).
3. Place your hands behind your head, and cross your right leg over your left as you arch your upper body over to the upper left corner of the mat (Photo 3).
4. Hold for three minutes, maintaining as much stillness as possible.

1

5. Build this position on the other side (Photos 4, 5, & 6).

6. Hold for an additional three minutes. You should feel the stretch in your side-body, although it may be a subtle sensation that you feel more on the release of the stretch than during the actual pose.

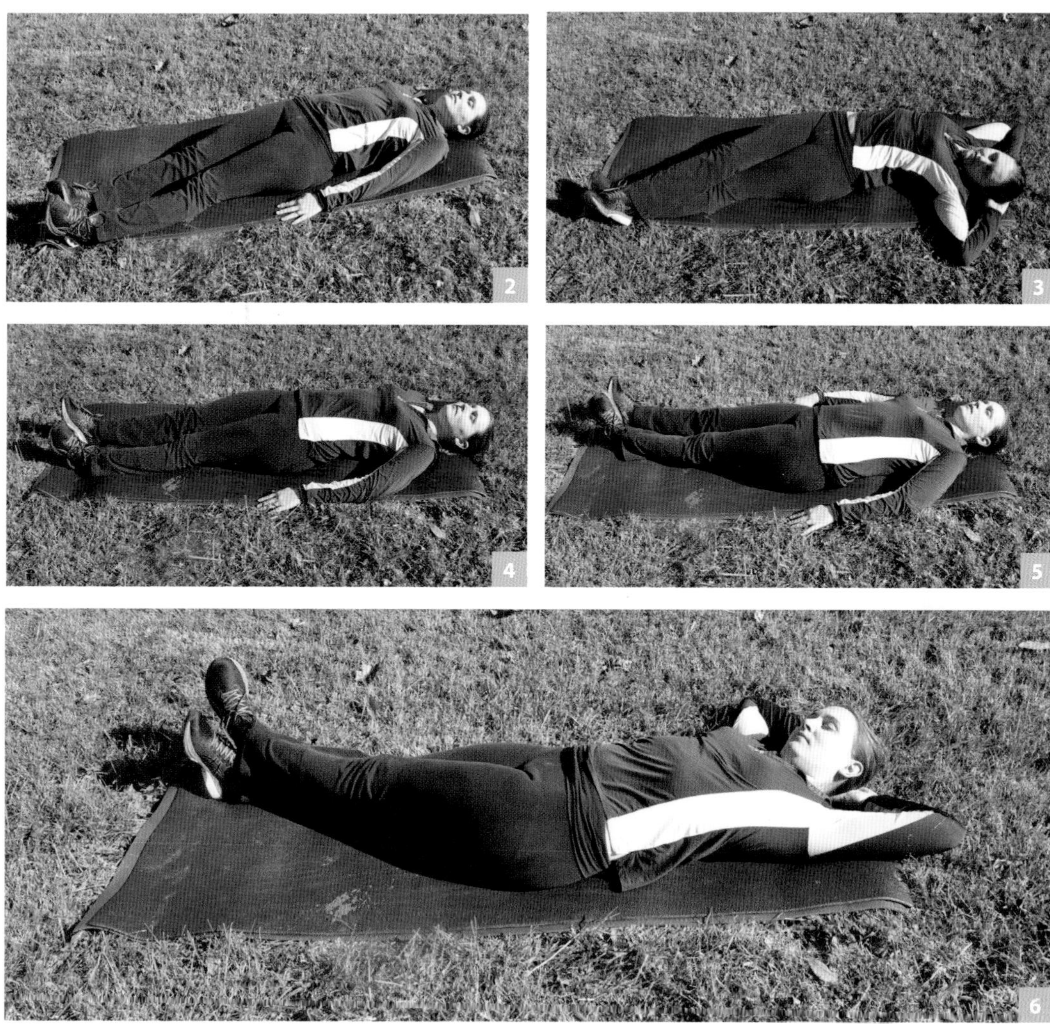

Cypress Knees

1. Lie on your back with your knees bent and your arms at your sides (Photo 1).
2. Thread your right foot through your bent left knee and, if you have the mobility, hold your right toes with your left hand (Photo 2).
3. Maintain this position for three minutes.
4. Build the pose to the other side by threading your left foot through your right bent leg and holding on to your left foot (only if this doesn't cause you to bend or twist to grab it). You should feel this in your quad and hip, though it may, like the last stretch, be a subtle sensation that you feel more on the release.

Supine Pigeon

1. Lie on your back with your knees bent, and place your right ankle on your left knee (Photo 1).

2. Lift your legs and clasp the back of your left thigh with your hands (Photo 2).

3. Relax into this position, your legs resting in your hands, as much as you can, for three minutes.

(continued)

1

2

4. Stretch the other side by placing your left ankle on your right knee and clasping the back of your right leg (Photos 3 & 4).

5. Hold for three minutes. You should feel this in your iliotibial (IT) band or the outside of your hip on the leg that is bent and placed against the other. (If this stretch is not accessible, do the Reclined Pigeon instead—see p. 103.)

3

4

Butterfly

1. Sit on your mat with knees relaxed out and the bottoms of your feet together (Photo 1).
2. Reach forward and clasp your ankles as you fold your torso forward over your legs. You can look straight ahead or look down at the ground (Photo 2).
3. Maintain this position for three minutes. You should feel the stretch in your inner thigh and in your lower back.

1

2

Mermaid Twist

1. Sit on your left hip next to your bolster (facing the long way) with your legs stacked upon each other (Photo 1).
2. Straddle the pillow with your hands, twist through your body, and lie down with your chest flat on the bolster (Photo 2).
3. Feel free to keep your head facing the same direction as your knees, but if it feels good in your neck (no sharp shooting sensation), turn your nose away from your bent legs and rest your head on the bolster facing the opposite direction (Photo 3).
4. Hold this position for three minutes.
5. Perform the stretch in the other direction and hold for three minutes. You should feel this stretch in your thoracic spine. This is a good pose to aid digestion (Photos 4, 5, and 6).

3

4

5

6

Supported Fish

1. Sit on your butt with your legs bent and the short side of the bolster against your back (Photo 1).
2. Lie back on the bolster and extend your legs out straight in front of you as your stretch your arms into a "T" position (Photo B).
3. Hold for three minutes. You should feel the stretch across your chest, and depending on how tight the fascia is, you may feel it in your lower back.

Conclusion

Riding horses is an all-consuming sport. It is important to know that you, as an equestrian, are an athlete.

The first pillar of any successful rider fitness program is *riding* as often as you can and as many different horses as you can. This is where you really learn the skills necessary to be successful in the tack.

The second pillar is *strength training*, which yields great results such as building muscle that supports whatever you choose to do on horseback. You will never be stronger than your horse, and that is not the goal, but added muscle on your body gives you the ability to be more accurate and precise with the aids that you are applying.

The third pillar of a rider fitness program is *stretching*. This is not just any stretching but long static holds that target the fascia that holds you together.

The fourth pillar is *rest and recovery*. This is a fundamental but often neglected part of any person's fitness program. You would not ride your horse for weeks or months on end without giving him a day off; however, oftentimes riders are so dedicated to the care and training program of their horses that their own bodies become afterthoughts. If you want riding to be a lifelong passion—like the Queen of England, who is still out riding at 94—you need to prioritize your rest and recovery, because injury and overuse will sideline you prematurely if you do not. This is why rest and recovery is not a suggestion, it is an integral pillar of a successful exercise program.

My experience has led me on a quest to find the ultimate fitness routine for riders. I found it interesting that top athletes in other sports across the board used cross-training, but when I asked equestrian professionals I looked up to about their fitness routines, they did not exist. My riding mentor as a child was eventually unable to ride because by the time she was 45, she suffered from excessive pain in her knees and lower back. When I started experiencing pain myself at a very young age, I knew that I had to course-correct or I would not be able to do the activity that I love more than anything else in the world for much longer. Improper biomechanics and always trying to fit more in the wheelbarrow or carrying heavy water buckets, along with being dumped repeatedly by naughty ponies, had given me the spine of a 90-year-old, I was told by a surgeon. Through physical therapy I was able to regain the strength I had lost and reduce my pain to a manageable level. I was able to continue riding, and today, at 30, I am in far better shape than I was at my athletic peak of 15. While I do have permanent damage that I will have to manage for the rest of my life, my experience lit a fire in me to share what I had learned in order to prevent others from going down a similar path.

> ***When you are a busy professional equestrian who is already burning the candle at both ends, you are already very active.***

One of my clients was a professional horsewoman who broke her ankle. It was a massive injury that required multiple surgeries and a lot of time off. Years after she had suffered the injury and rehabilitated it, she was still suffering from pain at the end of the day. She had a very active job so slowing down was not an option. However, the pain she experienced really made her consider a full career change. We started incorporating a single 30-minute exercise routine a week, and instead of having her work with me a second time, I encouraged her to take more advantage of her one day off a week. Instead of using her downtime to catch up on all her errands, I suggested she go grocery shopping on another day and taught her to value her rest and recovery. My client was hesitant at first, understandably so, but within three months she really started to notice a difference. Her usual pain had become more manageable; she even competed a little bit and was feeling more confident than ever in the tack.

The trick is to find what works with your schedule. When you are a busy professional equestrian who is already burning the candle at both ends, you are already very active. Exercising regularly is important to fill the imbalances that you develop on horseback; however, what is more important is that your support the third pillar (stretching), and the fourth pillar (rest and recovery). If you are a teenager or a person with a "nonhorse job," trying to balance a busy competition schedule with the demands of school, work, and life, you need to focus on the second pillar (strength training) because you really are not getting enough through riding one or two horses a day. If you are a weekend warrior, the biggest impact you will have on your riding will be by riding more—the first pillar of my exercise program.

This book is simply a guideline that you can follow. Remember that setbacks are a part of the process. We can't always be perfect, and perfection is actually the enemy of exercise programs because you have to be willing to suck a little first. You are trying something new, so you will not be the best at it. Stick with it through "the suck," and you will become proficient! The results will come with time. You have to stick with your exercise program for at least six weeks to start feeling the difference in the tack. Changes will be subtle at first—for example, you may notice after your show jumping course you have more gas in the tank. Or you will find your sitting trot feels more plugged in. Three months into this exercise program, you will notice that you are able to maintain your galloping position over a full cross-country course without feeling pain in your knees. You will no longer become breathless when you are riding a dressage test. Stick with it.

You can do it.

About the Author

Laura Crump Anderson is a lifelong equestrian who realized from an early age the importance of caring for riders' bodies like the athletes we expect our horses to be. At an early age, Laura ended up with a chronic overuse injury to her spine without ever having set foot in a gym. Through physical therapy, she was able to continue riding and caring for her horses. This experience inspired an interest in health and physical fitness.

Laura has a degree in Kinesiology with a concentration in Exercise Science. She is an American College of Sports Medicine Certified Personal Trainer and has also completed 200 hours of yoga teacher training. Upon graduating from school, Laura founded Hidden Heights Fitness and has worked with a wide range of athletes, from weekend warriors to former Olympians in the disciplines of dressage, eventing, and

© TYLIR RUSS

show jumping. Her favorite thing to do is help riders discover the strength to ride better than they ever thought possible or to help them regain former levels of activity and achievement after time off or an injury (hiddenheightsfitness.com).

Acknowledgments

This book has truly been a team effort. First off, I want to thank Trafalgar Square Books, because this book would not exist without their time, expertise, and dedication to producing a product worth reading. I would like to thank my editor Kate Adams, who has not only consistently believed in me but who spent hours of her time decoding my "Lauranese."

Thank you to my brother Mike, who dedicated so much of his time and put me through a fantastic writer's weekend to get me over a bout of writer's block.

I want to thank the countless riders who contributed their time to this book. While some of them are pictured in the photos, there are many others who have helped shape my philosophy of physical fitness for the equestrian.

I would like to thank my riding mentors: Sara Spofford, Jan Bynny, and Maggie Smith. Without them I would not be the horsewoman that I am today. I would like to name a few of the countless physical therapists and PTAs who taught me how exercise is medicine: Jill, Emily, Genny, Shaista, Purvi, Alli, Shruti, Mary, Catherine, Alison, Tara, Janell, Alastair, Sandy…and many more. Thank you to my yoga teacher Machelle Lee, who has taught me more about anatomy than a textbook ever could.

Thank you to my parents, who believed in a girl with a dream and have done their best to support that dream. I want to thank every single horse that has come into my life, and all the future horses, because I have never met a horse that was not an amazing teacher.

Lastly, I want to thank my incredible husband, who married a horse girl and continues to be my rock. I could not imagine navigating this crazy thing we call life without you.

Index

Page numbers in *italics* indicate illustrations.